MAKING SENSE OF
THE OLD TESTAMENT
LAW, PRIESTS,
SACRIFICES AND
FEASTS

Light in the Shadows

Ed Landry

AN EASY-TO-UNDERSTAND
BIBLE COMMENTARY

LIGHT IN THE SHADOWS
An easy-to-understand Bible Commentary series
Copyright © 2017 by Uplifting Christian Books

Published in Nashville, TN by Uplifting Christian Books
All rights reserved.
No part of this book may be reproduced in any written, electronic, recording, or photo-copying without written permission of the publisher or author. The exception would be in the case of brief quotations embodied in the critical articles or reviews and pages where permission is specifically granted by the publisher or author.

Scriptures marked AMP are taken from the AMPLIFIED BIBLE (AMP): Scripture taken from the AMPLIFIED® BIBLE, Copyright © 1954, 1958, 1962, 1964, 1965, 1987 by the Lockman Foundation Used by permission. (www.Lockman.org)

Scriptures marked HCSB are taken from the HOLMAN CHRISTIAN STANDARD BIBLE (HCSB): Scripture taken from the HOLMAN CHRISTIAN STANDARD BIBLE, copyright© 1999, 2000, 2002, 2003 by Holman Bible Publishers, Nashville Tennessee. All rights reserved.

Scriptures marked NLT are taken from the HOLY BIBLE, NEW LIVING TRANSLATION (NLT): Scriptures taken from the HOLY BIBLE, NEW LIVING TRANSLATION, Copyright© 1996, 2004, 2007 by Tyndale House Foundation. Used by permission of Tyndale House Publishers, Inc., Carol Stream, Illinois 60188. All rights reserved. Used by permission.

Scriptures marked KJV are taken from the KING JAMES VERSION (KJV): KING JAMES VERSION, public domain.

Scriptures marked NASB are taken from the NEW AMERICAN STANDARD (NAS): Scripture taken from the NEW AMERICAN STANDARD BIBLE®, copyright© 1960, 1962, 1963, 1968, 1971, 1972, 1973, 1975, 1977, 1995 by The Lockman Foundation. Used by permission

Scriptures marked NIV are taken from the NEW INTERNATIONAL VERSION (NIV): Scripture taken from THE HOLY BIBLE, NEW INTERNATIONAL VERSION ®. Copyright© 1973, 1978, 1984, 2011 by Biblica, Inc.™. Used by permission of Zondervan

Author - Ed Landry
Editorial team- Janet Landry and Rachel Butler
Book and cover design by the author
Artwork by David Landry.   http://www.th3anomaly.com/

ISBN-13: 978-0-9990931-0-8

Printed in the United States of America

Acknowledgements

It is hard to start naming names for fear of forgetting someone but there are a few key players in my life which have had a direct bearing on my love for the Old Testament and my desire to be a better teacher of the Bible. The short list of those who have influenced my understanding of the Shadows of the Cross are:

God. Of course He gets top billing. When we know the Author of the greatest book ever written it is amazing how much sense His book makes. His love changed my life forever and now I want others to know Him.

Dr. Ted Rendall. His classes on the Tabernacle aroused in me a deep interest in the topic. He helped me to not be afraid of the shadows.

Paul Maxwell. His heart for God and Spirit-filled teaching made me want to teach better and to touch lives. He was the first one to awaken my confused mind to the big issues of Law and Grace. He made me learn to love the shadows.

Pastor James Mader. His heart for the nation of Israel helped me love the people of the shadows.

Janet, my first and only wife. She is my sounding board, my kindest critic, my greatest encourager and continues to be the love of my life even after 50 years of marriage.

Thank you. Each of you are a part of this book. The good parts, of course. I will take the blame for the other parts.

Ed Landry

Recommendations

"The Old Testament: Tabernacle, temple, priests, animal sacrifices, festivals, the Law . . . What does all this stuff mean?! Wouldn't it be great to have a concise, clear, readable explanation in layman's terms filled with illustrations and charts for added clarity? Ed Landry has done this in "Light in the shadows." In nearly forty years of Bible Teaching ministry I have not seen a clearer or more concise overview of these Biblical subjects. Whether you are a new or older Christian, I highly recommend this book. You will understand the Old Testament and be filled with wonder at the beautiful portrait of Christ God painted through the Old Testament."

Dr. John Fernandez, Pastor of Grace Church of Napa Valley; Professor of theology at The Cornerstone Seminary in Vallejo Calif.

"Profound truth is best taught in simple ways. But simplicity is not to be confused with simple-mindedness. As great teachers do, Ed Landry puts the cookies where people like me can reach them, unpacking the truths of God's Word with clarity and purpose. This book is a great accomplishment and a great blessing to those of us needing direction and answers to questions that truly matter."

Phil Callaway, author and speaker

"God has used Ed Landry's sharp analytical mind to outline the marvelous unity of the Word of God. His panoramic view of Scripture shows how the shadows in the Old Testament types and symbols came to living reality in Christ's person and work. Ed's total unwavering commitment to Christ was illustrated in his victorious battle with cancer, and is now demonstrated in 'Light in the Shadows.'"

Paul Maxwell In 1970 Paul began teaching at Prairie Bible Institute and in 1978 became its president. From1989 to 2003 Paul served as president of International Student Ministries, Canada

"Ed Landry keeps things simple. The line drawings, charts and subtitles all help but it is the verbal illustrations and similes he uses that most clarify his subject for the average reader. I recommend this book for Christians who tend to back away from Old Testament chapters that deal with priests, feasts and ceremonies. Landry makes a good case for why they are relevant to us today."

Debbie Meroff (ICT- Operation MObilization's official journalist for past 20 years and published author.

"Finally, an enjoyable, user-friendly book about topics in the Old Testament that would normally make your nose bleed.

As a bible teacher, I must confess I did not fully understand these topics, nor did I have a strong inclination to understand them, owing to their cultural strangeness, complexity and burdensome detail. Landry's book makes what could be a life-changing journey comfortable and fun.

If you are a Christian, you will enjoy getting a better appreciation of God's amazing magnificence, integrity, and graciousness, as He unfolds His plan of salvation for man. If you are not a Christian, you will at least take away a clear understanding of the basis for the Christian faith. Either way, this book will definitely not waste your time. A highly recommended read."

Alex Castillo (Christian Leader and Bible teacher, Philippines)

"This is a well done basic presentation of OT typology around the tabernacle and think it would be of help to a new convert or as discipleship material. It is the kind of foundational material that will service believers for many years as they grow in faith."

L.L. (Don) Veinot Jr., (PresidentMidwest Christian Outreach, Inc.

CONTENTS

INTRODUCTION

Simple minded - in a good way

Recently, my wife and I visited a Shaker community in Eastern Kentucky. The Shakers were a religious community that was active 200 years ago. They based their lives on simplicity. Their furniture designs were like a refreshing breeze across the land. No clutter, no distraction, just simple beauty – that was the Shaker way.

The calmness, cleanness and restfulness that defined the Shaker environments reminds me of something other than architecture. I think of the way Jesus taught. His words were not like those of the Pharisees and Scribes, full of clutter and unnecessary pomp. They were simple and straight to the point, straight to the heart. He didn't fill his sentences with intellectual arguments, difficult vocabulary, high society poetry or complex theological arguments. The words of Jesus were breathtaking beauty in simplicity. For example, when discussing the kingdom of God, which is as vast as God Himself, He said:

> "... the kingdom of God is like ... a mustard seed, which is the smallest of all seeds on earth. Yet when planted, it grows and becomes the largest of all garden plants, with such big branches that the birds can perch in its shade." (Mark 4:30-32)

and,

> "It is like yeast that a woman took and mixed into about sixty pounds of flour until it worked all through the dough." (Luke 13: 21)

This is how He spoke to everyday people, in simple words and simple ideas, to help them grasp the bigger picture. Jesus wanted the people to understand. The Pharisees and teachers of the Law angered Jesus because they obscured God's message. They wanted to make themselves look and sound important. Listen to what Jesus said to them:

> "But woe to you, scribes and Pharisees, hypocrites, because you shut off the kingdom of heaven from people; for you do not enter in yourselves, nor do you allow those who are entering to go in." (Matthew 23:13)

Sometimes a person only needs the clear, short answer to get them over the frustration or misunderstanding they are struggling with. He spoke to fishermen and used fishing illustrations. When His audience was farmers and shepherds, He talked about the plants and fields when describing the Kingdom. When He met the woman at the well He spoke of water and used that to lead her to the Kingdom *(John 4)*.

The purpose of this book

This book will tackle the Old Testament sacrificial system, the law, the Tabernacle and Temple, the priests and the feasts of Israel. But unlike many books written on these subjects this one will be simple and clear. I personally struggled for years with those parts of the Bible. I am now writing the book I wished I had during those early struggles.

If Jesus were teaching a group of people today about these topics, I think He would do it in a simple and clear fashion. That was His style. You know what? I like His style! I think He would have liked the Shaker architecture.

The first section of this book will deal with three very important concepts that need to be always kept in mind when reading the Old Testament. I have given the first section a very profound title. It is called "Three Very Important Things." I told you this was going to be simple. Once we have looked at those three very important things we will begin our journey into the world of priests and sacrifices, feasts and laws and blood and stuff. Relax, it will all make sense. Let's get going.

Three Very Important Things

"For
I the Lord do
not change"

- Malachi 3:6 -

CHAPTER 1

Very Big Thing #1
GOD'S ONE UNCHANGING PLAN FOR ALL OF CREATION

One of the central teachings of the Bible about God is His unchangeableness. Theologians refer to this as His immutability. You and I change. We get old, we change views and learn things throughout life but God does not. He is the same perfect God today He was 20 bazillion years ago and will be the same perfect God forever. He is and always will be God.

Not only has God never changed, but His eternal purpose has never changed. When God created all things He knew exactly what He was doing and did exactly that. God never changes His mind, never makes a mistake.

> **"He who is the Glory of Israel does not lie or change his mind; for he is not a human being, that he should change his mind."**
> (1 Samuel 15:29)

God is also all-knowing. Did you ever think about the fact that God never learns anything? He never says, " I never knew that!" He just knows and always has and always will.

When it comes to understanding the Old Testament these two attributes of God (along with all of God's other attributes of course), give us a very important hint to help us in our study. Since God knows it all and He never changes we can rightly assume that He has had one unchanging plan from the beginning when He created everything. Before Creation ever began, God knew what was coming. God knew the fall of mankind would happen before a single person walked in the garden. He knew the only solution for His soon to be broken creation would be a personal intervention. God would one day have to come to His spoiled planet Himself and become one of us and provide the one and only solution that could fix the problem.

That was all known before God spoke everything into existence. The solution, as we now know, was the incarnation of God the Son into humanity, Jesus. Out of love God created and it was His love that drove God the Son to the cross to pay the eternal price for the eternal damage we had done as His wayward children. Jesus is referred to in Scripture as the "Lamb slain from the foundation of the earth." The death and resurrection of Christ is God's one unchanging plan for all of creation. It was His plan before He spoke the universe into existence and it remains His same plan today. He always knew it and it has never changed.

So why is this so important in helping us read the Old Testament? For many the New Testament makes sense but the Old

Testament sounds like a different story. The New Testament is about Jesus, the church and the people of God. It is about love and grace. Some view the Old Testament as a book about law and God's anger. It is viewed as a dark spot in history, a time when man sought to appease the wrath of God with animal sacrifices and lived in a mire of religious ceremonies and priests and rules and regulations. It almost sounds like two different stories, two different peoples and even two different Gods. At least God, some think, treated the people differently then than He does today.

OK, a few deep breaths now

Back to what we know again. God knows and always has known it all from beginning to the end and God never changes. He has had one eternal plan from the beginning and we are still under that plan, as all men have been from the beginning. The Old Testament and the New Testament are the history of that one unchanging plan of God.

When we read the first few chapters of God's Word we discover the Creation, the Fall, and the Curse. When we read the last few chapters of the Book of Revelation, we note all the problems are solved and curses removed. The following list suggests a few of the loose ends that are taken care of by God when He closes the pages of His book:

Genesis . . .	Revelation . . .
Man falls in sin	Man resurrected, sin is no more
Death enters creation	Death forever removed
Fallen earth and universe	New resurrected Earth and new heavens
Satan seizes dominion of earth	Satan removed, judged, God is Lord and King
God in heaven separated from man	God on earth living with man
The curse	No more curse, greater blessing than even before
Man in shame	No more shame
Tree of life cut off from man	Tree of life in New Jerusalem, man has access
God obscured because of man's sin	God seen in his Glory
Relationships tainted by sin	Perfect relationships
Man and animals at odds	Man and beast live in harmony
Ground cursed	Ground fertile
Starvation and drought	Abundant food and water
Toil in labor, restlessness	Enhanced restfulness, joy in labor
Paradise lost	Paradise regained, magnified
Clothed due to unrighteousness	Man clothed in Righteousness

(adapted from Heaven by Randy Alcorn)

God knows how to finish a book! And what a book it is. It is one story; it is the same story. That story is the cross of Christ. Both the Old and the New are about that one story, the love story of God and His rebellious people, both then and now.

New and old, same story told

Both Testaments point to the very same historical point on the timeline of humanity, the cross. Both Testaments present the way of salvation as grace through faith. That is how all people have found eternal life at any time in human history. The story never changed because God never changed. The center of human history is where the love of God and the sin of man meet. It is the cross where Jesus died for our sins to reconcile us back to God. The cross is the focal point of the entire Bible. The Old Testament points ahead to it, and the New Testament points back to it.

> **"The New is in the Old contained**
> **The Old is in the New explained"**
> (attributed to Augustine)

But if Jesus had not yet been born how did people living then understand the one unchaning plan of redemption? If man was to find eternal life based on grace through faith what were all those animal sacrifices and priests and feasts for in the old times? Those are great questions. They lead to the second of the three very important things we need to understand.

"Because God wanted to make the unchanging nature of his purpose very clear to the heirs of what was promised, he confirmed it with an oath."

Hebrews 6:17

e you ever wondered?Have you eve
dered?Have you ever wondered?H
ever wondered?Have you ever won
dered?Have you ever wondered?H
ever wondered?Have you ever won
dered?Have you ever wondered?H

- What the Covenants were
and why God made them?

- Why are Abraham and David
given such
importance in the
Bible?

CHAPTER 2

Very Big Thing #2
GOD'S TWO-FOLD PROGRAM

One of the great traditional Christmas hymns is Joy to the World. No doubt we have all heard the following words:

> **"No more let sins and sorrows grow,**
> **Nor thorns infest the ground;**
> **He comes to make His blessings flow**
> **Far as the curse is found,**
> **Far as the curse is found,**
> **Far as, far as, the curse is found."**

As far as the curse is found. It's true. The redemptive work of Christ on the cross is all encompassing. His sacrificial death and victorious resurrection announced to every square inch of the universe that the end of the curse was a certainty. Once this final chapter of earth's history plays out and God makes a new heaven and new earth, we are guaranteed that the curse will not be part of that new creation ever again. Until that time we are still part of what the Scripture refers to as the groaning creation.

> "Yet what we suffer now is nothing compared to the glory he will reveal to us later. [19] For all creation is waiting eagerly for that future day when God will reveal who his children really are. [20] Against its will, all creation was subjected to God's curse. But with eager hope, [21] the creation looks forward to the day when it will join God's children in glorious freedom from death and decay. [22] For we know that all creation has been groaning as in the pains of childbirth right up to the present time. [23] And we believers also groan, even though we have the Holy Spirit within us as a foretaste of future glory, for we long for our bodies to be released from sin and suffering. We, too, wait with eager hope for the day when God will give us our full rights as his adopted children." (Romans 8:18-23)

I don't know about you but I am really looking forward to that day.

When man chose darkness over the light the losses were beyond calculation. He lost his intimate relation with his maker. Sin drove a wedge between God and man. The earth itself went from user friendly to complete hostility. The environment and animal kingdom became enemies. Everything has been at war ever since. The earth was handed over to enemy control. Everything is broken!

Satan is now the "Prince and power of the air." "The whole

world lies in the hands of the evil one." The entire human race was plunged into slavery to sin. This is all part of the Fall and the Curse. The kingdom God made was fractured and is now occupied by enemy forces. The entire universe squirms in agony awaiting the final resurrection when the curse, along with sin and death, will be eternally removed from those who trust in God.

Meanwhile, God set in motion from the beginning a two-fold rescue plan often referred to as Redemption and Kingdom. Redemption refers to His plan for man and Kingdom refers primarily to His reign and rule over all things. When Jesus came the first time He paid the price of redemption. He bought us back from the slave market of sin. He, the King of Kings and Lord of Lords, willingly died as a sacrifice for our sin. And one day He is coming again to get His people and His stuff. He is our Redeemer and He is our King.

> **"This is what the LORD says—**
> **Israel's King and Redeemer, the LORD Almighty:**
> **I am the first and I am the last;**
> **apart from me there is no God."**
> (Isaiah 44:6)

Even though God has allowed an enemy to exercise authority over the domain we live in, God is still the ultimate King and controller of all things. Even though there will be an actual time when Christ begins an eternal rule on a new earth, He is still King of Kings now. When we discuss these issues of redemption and kingdom they are being used in a general sense, there is always some overlap. They are two aspects of His one great plan.

For God to solve the problem caused by the Fall He needed to deal with two major issues, restoring fallen man and reclaiming His besieged Kingdom. What He set up in the Old Testament was a shadow, a temporary system designed to show man that his help came from outside of himself and that God would one day send the final solution. It looked like this drawing:

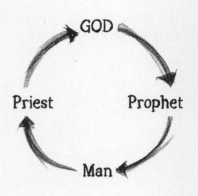

Man understood from this system that God spoke to man through the prophets and man had access to God through the priests. A mediator was necessary. Man in his sinful condition was separated from God by an infinite chasm. One day that chasm would be bridged, but until then man had to trust God, have faith in His solution. When Jesus arrived on the scene, He came as the final prophet, spokesman for God and the ultimate mediator. After the death and resurrection of Christ, no human offices of Priest and Prophet were necessary for man to communicate with or have access to God. Jesus bridged it all.

Two great rivers run though the Bible

Throughout the Old Testament all prophecy points to either God's Redemptive plan or His Kingdom plan. The Old Testament types and promises were either about Redemption or Kingdom. They are like two great rivers flowing from Genesis to Revelation. All along the river there are streams and waterfalls that add more and more to the river. Our knowledge grows with each new revelation God gives us. We will talk more about this in the next chapter when we discuss progressive revelation and types, the pictures God sent before He sent the person.

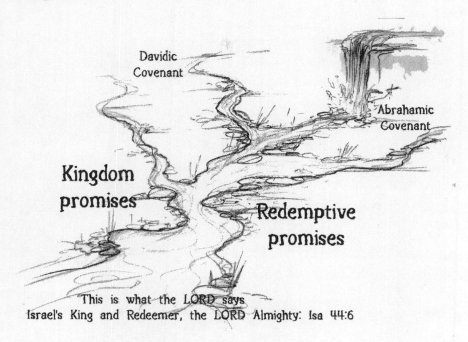

Davidic Covenant

Abrahamic Covenant

Kingdom promises

Redemptive promises

"This is what the LORD says Israel's King and Redeemer, the LORD Almighty: Isa 44:6

The redemptive promises of God came though Abraham. We refer to this as the Abrahamic Covenant. His son, Isaac, was a picture of substitution and sacrifice and grace. The Kingdom promises came through the line of David, or Davidic Covenant. His son, Solomon, was Israel's greatest king and pictured the final King of Kings that would also come through David's line.

The chart on the next page is meant to show the two distinct purposes of God. It doesn't mean David had no redemptive promises, he did. But the primary promise to David points to the One who will sit on the final throne as King and Ruler. And the primary promise to Abraham pointed to the One who would one day bless the nations. He would be the Saviour, the Redeemer. All the prophecies pointed to one person who would fulfill both the redemptive and kingdom purposes of God

The Lion and the Lamb - God's Two-fold Program

Two Purposes	Redemption reclaiming fallen man	Kingdom Restoring God's rightful rule
Two Covenants	Abraham	David
Two Sons	Isaac, the perfect sacrifice	Solomon the great king
Two Animals	Lamb	Lion
Two Emblems	Cross	Crown
Two Comings	Suffering Servant (1st coming)	Reigning King (2nd coming)
Two Administrations	Savior Grace	Lord Law

These two great themes run from Genesis to Revelation. When we get to the final heavenly scene at the throne of God the book of Revelation tells about an angel looking for one worthy to open the scroll. He hears that the Lion from the tribe of Judah is worthy and he looks and sees a lamb that has been slain. The two streams flow out of Genesis, weave their way throughout the Scriptures and finally come together at the throne of God. He is the Lion and Lamb, King and Redeemer, the Beginning and the End. He redeems, he rules.

We often think of the New Testament beginning with the soft
cry of a baby in a manger. But actually the first few words of
the New Testament are more like the roar of a great waterfall.
The Old Testament had been a sequence of gathering streams
of Kingdom and Redemptive promises. It became a mighty
river of prophecy. One was coming who was both King and
Redeemer. One was coming who was both son of David and son
of Abraham. Now, listen to the roar of the first verse of the New
Testament.

Matthew 1:1

A record of
the genealogy
of Jesus Christ

the son of
David, the son
of Abraham

When the New Testament begins we have our first introduc-
tion to the person of Jesus Christ, the promise of God, the hope
of the ages and the fulfillment of God's two-fold program.

Jesus was the answer to the promise God made to King David
that the Kingdom would be restored through his line.

The Davidic Covenant

> **"Your house and your kingdom will endure forever
> before me:
> your throne will be established forever.' "**
> (2 Samuel 7:16)

And Jesus was the answer to the promise that God made to Abraham that the Redemption would come through his line. God would bless the world through Abraham.

The Abrahamic Covenant

> **"I will bless those who bless you,
> and whoever curses you I will curse;
> and all peoples on earth
> will be blessed through you."**
> (Genesis 12:3)

The reason there were these two primary covenants was that God was dealing with two primary issues. When Jesus is introduced in the New Testament as the fulfillment of these two covenants God is saying that Jesus is the answer to the two main issues God has been addressing throughout all time, those things relating to Redemption and those things relating to his Kingdom. Jesus had come for His people, to be our Savior and for His stuff, to be the rightful ruler.

It is amazing what is found in the shadows. It is there where the light appears the brightest.

Now it is time to lay one more critical foundation stone, the third of the very important things that give us the lenses to properly understand the Old Testament. After that we will head to a mountain where God laid down the Law.

e you ever wondered?Have you eve
dered?Have you ever wondered?H
ever wondered?Have you ever wor
dered?Have you ever wondered?H
ever wondered?Have you ever wor
dered?**Have you ever wondered?**H

- Why God used lambs, altars and priests to show man the way to faith?

- Why didn't he just tell the people they needed faith? Why set up such an elaborate system?

CHAPTER 3

Very Big Thing #3

PREVIEWS OF THE COMING ATTRACTION

I imagine most of the readers of this book have at some time seen a movie in a theatre. Before the movie begins, it is traditional (and good marketing) to show previews of movies that are not yet released but coming soon. And sometimes the previews give a fairly good idea of what the upcoming movies are all about. That is what God did for those living in Old Testament times. He gave them an amazing preview of the coming attraction. Then the book of Hebrews in the New Testament reminded the people that the main feature had finally opened and they didn't need to keep watching the previews any longer. That same book of Hebrews reveals to us just how God presented those previews to those who lived before Christ came.

> "In the past God spoke to our forefathers through the prophets at many times and in various ways, 2but in these last days he has spoken to us by his Son, whom

**he appointed heir of all things, and through whom he
made the universe."**
(Hebrews 1:1:2) `

Let's read that same passage in the Amplified Bible

**"IN MANY separate revelations (each of which set
forth a portion of the Truth) and in different ways
God spoke of old to [our] forefathers in and by the
prophets, [2][But] in the last of these days He has spoken to us in [the person of a] Son, Whom He appointed Heir and lawful Owner of all things, also by and
through Whom He created the worlds and the reach-
es of space and the ages of time [He made, produced,
built, operated, and arranged them in order]."**
(The Amplified Bible, Hebrews 1:1,2)

What this tells us is that God used two different ways to communicate His plan of redemption through the cross to the
people who lived before Christ was born. He did it by using a
variety of object lessons and He also revealed the information
progressively over time with each new revelation increasing
in detail. It is important that we briefly examine each of these
methods. The stories recorded in the Old Testament are not
just random events but are given to us with a purpose in mind.

The first method of communication we will look at is God's
use of object lessons. He didn't just have His prophets and
teachers tell or proclaim information but he used "different
ways" to make sure man understood the message. God orches-
trated many different object lessons or visual aids to teach
man what his needs were and how he could be brought back

into right relationship with his Maker. God calls them a "type" when the object lesson teaches something about Christ.

Just my type

An example of God calling something a "type" is recorded in the book of Hebrews when it talks about Abraham being called by God to offer his son, Isaac, as a sacrifice.

> **"It was he to whom it was said, "IN ISAAC YOUR DE-SCENDANTS SHALL BE CALLED." [19]He considered that God is able to raise people even from the dead, from which he also received him back as a type."**
> (NASB, Hebrews 11:18, 19)

Types were Gods' previews of the coming attraction, the cross. Here is a good definition of a type

> *"A Type is an Old Testament institution, event, person, object, ceremony, or office, which has reality and purpose in biblical history, but which also by Divine design foreshadows something yet to be revealed."*
> D.K. Campbell

A type was either something that happened historically, an aspect of a person's life or an event that God used to illustrate something about the coming Savior. A type is always about Christ and God's great plan.

Here are examples of each of the categories from the definition.

1. An Institution that was designed by God as a type

- In the Jewish feast of the Passover God showed the people that the blood of a lamb protected their house from a coming judgment.

> **"Get rid of the old yeast that you may be a new batch without yeast—as you really are. For Christ, our Passover lamb has been sacrificed."** (1 Corinthians 5:7)

- The Jewish feast of First Fruits was a picture of the resurrection of Christ

> **"But now Christ has been raised from the dead, the first fruits of those who are asleep."**
> (1 Corinthians 15:20)

2. A Person could be used as a type

- Adam, as the beginning of the human race, is used by God to show that Christ is the beginning of a new race, the family of God.

> **"For as in Adam all die, so in Christ all will be made alive."** (1 Corinthians 15:22)

- God sometimes used people to present pictures of the coming Messiah and what He would do. People like Moses and Isaac. Another interesting person used as a type was Melchizedek (Genesis 14, Hebrews 7). He was an actual king of Salem (usually understood to be Jerusalem). Melchizedek also was the official priest of the area so he had a dual role as both ruler of his kingdom and spiritual leader of his people. He pictured Jesus our Great High

Priest and King of Kings. An interesting part of the type is that the Scripture intentionally does not record the ancestry of Melchizedek. He had a father and mother but we don't know anything about them. The Savior Melchizedek would picture, the Lord Jesus Christ, would come from eternity. As God, He had no beginning.

3. Some Events were also used by God to predict future events involving Christ.

- Jonah's experience in the great fish was a type of the resurrection of Christ. Jonah ran from God and his disobedience put an entire ship and crew at risk (Jonah 1). They tossed him overboard and as he sank to the depths of the sea he was swallowed up by a giant fish. He lay in that fish for three days and nights as in a tomb. Then after three days he was brought back to the land of the living and spit out on the shore. He then went on to preach the message God had given him in the first place. His three-day entombment and "resurrection" was later used by Jesus Himself to predict and describe His own resurrection.

> **"For as Jonah was three days and three nights in the belly of a huge fish, so the Son of Man will be three days and three nights in the heart of the earth."**
> (Matthew 12:40)

- The Exodus contained several types.
(1 Corinthians chapter 10)

4. Objects were often used to teach the people of God a great spiritual lesson about His plan for man.

- The Brazen Serpent. In Numbers chapter 21 we read a fascinating story. The children of Israel were being led by Moses across the wilderness when they became weary of the journey and began to grumble and complain against God. As a judgment God sent poisonous snakes into their midst and they bit many people and they died. No human remedy could be found for the snake bites.

So the people repented and cried out to Moses to ask God to remove the snakes. But God's response seemed quite unusual. He commanded Moses to make a serpent of bronze and put it on a pole and have it lifted it up above the camp. God then told them that when anyone was bitten they only had to look at the bronze serpent by faith and they would live.

Jesus, later in the New Testament, told Nicodemus that he needed to be born again and He explained what that meant by saying to him, "Just as Moses lifted up the snake in the desert, so the Son of Man must be lifted up, that everyone who believes in him may have eternal life." (John 3:14.15)

The bronze serpent in the Old Testament was a picture or type of the death of Christ and salvation.

God made him who had no sin to be sin for us, so that in him we might become the righteousness of God.
(2 Corinthians 5:21)

- Water poured from the rock after Moses struck it with his rod. This pictured the one who would be their Living Water. The New Testament recounts that event and says **"That Rock was Christ"** (1 Corinthians 10:4).

5. The Ceremonies of Israel had messianic meaning and instruction.

- The Whole Burnt Offering pictured the work of Christ on the cross. He gave himself completely.

- The Feasts of Israel depicted both of Christ's roles as Savior and as King of Kings and Lord of Lords.

6. Offices

God established the offices of Prophet, Priest and King to point to the One who is ultimately our final Prophet, our Great High Priest and the King of Kings. So, types are visual aids and object lessons God used to teach spiritual lessons to His people. Why did He do that? Abraham is a good example of why. God could have told Abraham, "Abraham, you are going to have a lot of children." But instead He told Abraham to look up at the stars which served as a reminder of His promise that a great family would come from him. Then He told him to look down and try to count the grains of sand. Abraham lived in the desert where all about him was only sand and stars. So God, in essence, by using a visual aid was showing Abraham both day and night that His promise was sure and immense. God does this throughout the Bible and so we should expect that when He wanted to communicate the greatest story in the universe he would use the best visual aids. And that is what He did.

The second way God communicated His great eternal truths about His Son was by progressive revelation. Let's look at that now.

Time after time

The book of Hebrews teaches that God used "MANY separate revelations (each of which set forth a portion of the Truth)" to unveil his message.

This is commonly referred to as progressive revelation. In other words God not only used object lessons but he also unveiled some lessons over a period of time. Each time he revealed

Adam	Abel	Abraham
Sin requires death	Lamb for sin	Lamb for a man

more and more until He was finished with what He was intending to teach. When we read through Scripture it is like watching a photograph in the developing solution become clearer and clearer until we finally see the fully developed image.

The greatest visual aid of all time, which told of God's plan for man's redemption, was the Tabernacle. It was the final developed photo of Christ in the Old Testament. We will spend several chapters on this topic but for now lets' look at the image of the lamb in Scripture as revealed by progressive revelation. Progressively through time God revealed more and more about the sacrificial lamb.

The Lamb in Scripture

"Behold the Lamb of God which takes away

Moses   Aaron

Lamb for a family   Lamb for a nation   the sin of the world"
John 1:29

Explaining the chart

- Adam understood that his sin separated him from his God. He also understood that death came into the world because of sin. The first death in Scripture is caused by Adam's sin.

- Abel was taught by his parents to offer a lamb on an altar to cover his sin and find forgiveness.

- Abraham understood more than Adam. He understood that a male ram was needed to be a substitute to satisfy the demands of God.

- When we arrive at the Levitical system in the time of Moses the picture is almost complete. A full sacrificial system is in place with priests, feasts and laws. It all points to the final sacrifice God will one day provide.

- The final frame was unveiled when John the Baptist saw Jesus and announced, "Behold the Lamb of God who takes away the sin of the world."

In those shadows and images one could always see an image of a man, God's man, who would one day come to earth to take away sin forever.

The shadows all led to a cross on a lonely hill. We will shortly take a tour of the Tabernacle, the house that God built. But before we get to that we need to take a look at a subject that is often confusing, the Law of God.

ve you ever wondered?Have you eve
idered?Have you ever wondered?H
ever wondered?Have you ever wor
idered?Have you ever wondered?H
ever wondered?Have you ever wor
idered?Have you ever wondered?H

- How were people saved before Jesus died on the Cross?

CHAPTER 4

God's Old Testament Picture Show
HE SENT A PICTURE BEFORE HE SENT THE PERSON

So we have begun with three very important things. 1. God has never changed. 2 His one unchanging plan is about Kingdom and Redemption. He came to save His people and He is coming back to get His stuff. 3. God communicated this plan to man in the Old Testament by numerous types and object lessons, and He did it over a period of time making them clearer and clearer as time progressed.

The entire Bible is very clear that salvation has always been by grace through faith. This was taught by the Law and Prophets. Salvation was never achieved by keeping the Law nor was it ever intended that way.

Here is what we read in Romans about the Old Testament and salvation:

"²¹**But now righteousness from God, apart from
law, has been made known, to which the Law and
the Prophets testify. ²²This righteousness from God
comes through faith in Jesus Christ to all who believe.
There is no difference, ²³for all have sinned and fall
short of the glory of God.**" (Romans 3:21-23)

The book of Hebrews also deals extensively with this subject. It was written to new believers in the first century who were trying to understand how the ceremonial law related to salvation by faith in Christ. Basically the entire book tells these first century believers that the entire Old Testament ceremonial law foreshadowed the cross of Christ. The book tells how the priests showed man he needed help to reach God and that the high priest was the ultimate mediator. Jesus is the final high priest to whom it all pointed.

The Old Testament high priest was a picture of Christ, our final sacrifice and High Priest. Hebrews takes its readers through the shadows of the Old Testament sacrificial system and reveals that they lead to the foot of the cross. The writer then explains that now that Christ has finally and fully come, the old system has finished its work. The shadow is no longer necessary. In other words God sent a picture before He sent a person. And what a picture it was. It was actually an entire photo album of His Son.

Man was never left without light even when he was in the shadows.

"**The old system under the law of Moses was only a
shadow, a dim preview of the good things to come,
not the good things themselves. The sacrifices under**

that system were repeated again and again, year after year, but they were never able to provide perfect cleansing for those who came to worship."
(Hebrews 10:1)

So if the Old Testament sacrifices could not save and were never meant to save, then how were people saved before Jesus came?

"What is faith? It is the confident assurance that what we hope for is going to happen. It is the evidence of things we cannot yet see. God gave his approval to people in days of old because of their faith."
(Hebrews 11:1, 2)

That is how God gave His approval in the days of old. It was always faith in God, not keeping a ritual or religious practice. That faith was based on the promise God gave to send a Savior and God does not break His oath. In a sense, man was saved on credit before Christ came. His salvation was real, simply by having faith in God to forgive him. That forgiveness was based on the work of Christ yet to come but it was guaranteed by God Himself.

We will shortly take a tour of the Tabernacle, the house that God built. But before we get to that we need to undeerstand the Law of God.

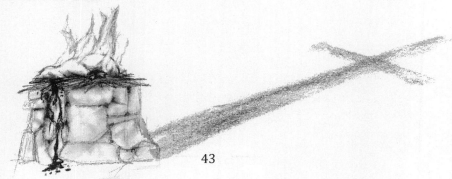

SECTION 2

It's the Law

The next three chapters in this section will help you better understand the issues and concepts regarding the Law of God and the grace of God. For many, the topic of law and grace is confusing and hard to reconcile. Was man saved in the Old Testament times by keeping the Law of God? Why did God give mankind a law no man could keep? How did man find eternal life before Jesus Christ was born? Was it a different system than it is today? Some see the Old Testament as law and the New Testament as grace. Is that right? What was the Law and why did God give it? These and other questions will be answered as we move along on our journey. We will begin with discovering what makes the law so confusing.

CHAPTER 5

Law and Order

WHY IS THE LAW SO DIFFICULT TO UNDERSTAND?

The word "law" is a simple word. However, it has so many definitions in the Bible that it is easy to be confused about which meaning is in view when it is used. Here are 14 specific uses of the word "law" found in Scripture:

1. WRITINGS OF MOSES, PENTATEUCH

Sometimes the word means the first five books of the Old Testament, the Pentateuch. Jesus, among others, used it in this way at times.

2. CEREMONIAL ORDINANCES OF THE MOSAIC LAW (LEVITICUS)

Sometimes the "law" is used to refer to the order and processes involved in the Levitical sacrificial system. Example – the laws of the offerings.

3. THE MORAL LAW

The word can mean what God expects of man in a general sense.

4. THE TEN COMMANDMENTS

5. UNIVERSAL PRINCIPLE LIKE THE LAW OF GRAVITY

A uniformly acting principle which governs an action. An example would be Paul talking about the "law of sin and death." It is a principle.

6. THE WRITINGS OF THE OLD TESTAMENT PROPHETS

Isaiah in particular.

7. JEWISH SYSTEM OF MINUTE REQUIREMENTS

These were mostly a misinterpretation of the true law. Included are Jewish traditions. A distorted system of law Israel had developed which contained hundreds of requirements for Israelites to do in order to find their way to God. This "law" was a burden no man could bear.

8. THE PSALMS

9. UNIQUE LAWS OR SYSTEM

Paul refers to the "law of Christ." This was in contrast to the Jewish system. It was a unique system of liberty, not bondage. Also included in this usage would be the precept concerning love.

10. SPECIFIC CIVIL LAW

Like a traffic law, a statute in government, precepts and injunctions.

11. LAWS IN GENERAL (LAW OF THE LAND)

Anything established or anything received by usage, a custom or a command.

12. OLD TESTAMENT AS A WHOLE

13. SELF-MADE SYSTEM OF WORKS TO EARN RIGHTEOUSNESS

The New Testament is very clear that no one is saved by "the works of the Law".

14. SPECIFIC LEGAL JURISDICTION

Example, the "law of the husband."

Now you see why it is so easy to be confused when we see the word "law."

Let's look at an example

Here is an example, of this challenge, from the New Testament. This short passage from Romans 7 uses the Greek word ***nomos*** (law) seven times but most of the usages describe different things.

> "So I find this <u>law</u> at work: When I want to do good, evil is right there with me. [22]For in my inner being I delight in God's <u>law</u>; [23]but I see another <u>law</u> at work in the members of my body, waging war against the <u>law</u> of my mind and making me a prisoner of the <u>law</u> of sin at work within my members. [24]What a wretched

man I am! Who will rescue me from this body of death? ²⁵Thanks be to God—through Jesus Christ our Lord! So then, I myself in my mind am a slave to God's law, but in the sinful nature a slave to the law of sin."
(Romans 7:21-25)

Notice each of the different meanings of the "law" in this passage:

- **"This law"** (verse 21) is talking about a general guiding principle. It is not talking about the ten commandments or the Old Testament writings.

- **"God's law"** (verse 22) The revealed Word of God, Old Testament Scriptures. Same as saying " I delight in the Word of God."

- **"another law"** (verse 23) A system of the flesh within a man, which wars with the holy revealed demands of God.

- **"law of my mind"** (verse 23) Our minds are strongly influenced by sin and its decisions are ruled by this corrupted entity.

- **"law of sin"** (verse 23) A universal constant like the law of gravity.

- **"Slave to God's law"** (versee 25) The righteous requirements of God.

- **"Slave to the law of sin."** (vefse 25) Same usage as number 5.

Whether you agree with each of these seven interpretations is not the point of this exercise. I just want to point out why the word "law" is sometimes confusing. It has a lot of uses in the Bible. The Greek word "nomos" and its five forms are used almost 200 times in the New Testament.

This book focuses on the word "law" as it relates to how God provided a solution to the sin problem of man. We will look at the big picture of what God communicated to man and how, in our sinful state, we can find our way back to God. This "law" that God has given man was intended to:

1. Expose our sin and bring us to repentance (Redemption).

2. Show us the way back to a right relationship with Him (Kingdom, His rule over us).

The main thing to get out of this chapter is that the subject of the law can be confusing and that we will be examining what is probably the most important usage of the word. God gave the "Law" to man to expose his need and show him the path that leads to eternal life.

ve you ever wondered?Have you eve
idered?Have you ever wondered?H
ever wondered?Have you ever wol
idered?Have you ever wondered?H
ever wondered?Have you ever wol
idered?Have you ever wondered?H

- Why "the Law" seems so restrictive and demanding?

CHAPTER 6

The Stone Judge
WHY GOD GAVE THE TEN COMMANDMENTS

The law often conjures up a very austere view of God. After all, he has "laid down the law." It sounds unbending, unmerciful, rigid, black and white and final. For some the word "law" means don't do this or don't do that. It is restrictive, prohibitive. What does the word "law" mean to you?

God must be stern, the celestial killjoy who enforces and punishes. He is the lawgiver, judge and executioner. Maybe we wouldn't use all those terms in the same sentence but some of these thoughts are not that uncommon. The law seems far removed from our understanding of the love of God. But you will find that it is totally consistent with the love and grace of God.

The meanings of "Law" that we will be focusing on are those usages that describe what God has done to bring His rebellious race back to Himself. So we will be looking at:

- The moral code, the Ten Commandments, and
- The Old Testament ceremonial system or Levitical system

As we look closely at them we will learn that they spring from the love of God and we will see why he gave them and what they have to do with us today.

Big losers

When man chose to sin and follow Satan rather than his maker he forfeited several things. He lost his relationship with God and he turned the earth over to God's arch enemy, Satan. Since then "the whole world lies in the power of the evil one" (1 John 5:19). God has always had a two-fold plan to remedy this two-fold problem. God wants to get His people back and to get His stuff back. We will develop this more in future chapters.

Remember "Very Big Thing #2" about Kingdom and Redemption? That is God's two fold plan- Redemption (God getting His people back) and Kingdom (God getting His stuff back.) "The Law" He gave man has to do with both Redemption and Kingdom. Throughout the Bible, God's promises and prophesies revolve around this two-fold program as well. Redemption is about fallen man getting into proper relationship with God. Kingdom is about man becoming part of God's eternal reign. The moral law shows man his need of redemption. The ceremonial law shows man the way back to God.

Let's begin with the moral law. God really only gave mankind two commandments. We are to love God and we are to love our neighbor. That's it. All the other laws, commands, judgments and statutes in the Bible originate from these two.

Jesus clarified this:

"Hearing that Jesus had silenced the Sadducees, the Pharisees got together. [35]One of them, an expert in the law, tested him with this question: [36]"Teacher, which is the greatest commandment in the Law?" [37]Jesus replied: " 'Love the Lord your God with all your heart and with all your soul and with all your mind.' [38]This is the first and greatest commandment. [39]And the second is like it: 'Love your neighbor as yourself.' [40]**All the Law and the Prophets hang on these two commandments."** Matthew 22:34-39, emphasis mine)

These are God's commandments and we have broken both of them. Our sin has driven a wedge between us and God. And our sinful nature keeps us from loving our neighbor as ourselves. It shouldn't surprise us that these two commandments are about loving God and loving each other. After all God is love so why wouldn't His hope for man be about love? But we need help to make it happen.

Total exposure

The Ten Commandments were an amplification of the two primary commandments. The first four commandments are about loving God and the last six are about how to treat our neighbor. If we love God we will not have other gods, profane His name or neglect our time with Him. If we love our neighbor we won't cheat him or steal from him, kill him, take his wife, etc. That is the basic moral law. Love God and love our neighbor as ourselves.

The big question is if God knew we couldn't keep the moral law why did He give it? One of the main reasons was to expose our true heart condition to us. The Law is like a mirror that shows us our sin. The Law is a teacher that instructs us. The lesson is a penetrating, clear reflection of what we really are. We are sinners and unable to rescue ourselves. The moral law was never given to help man stay on the right path. It showed man just how far he was off course. So the Law shows us we have broken it. Great, now what? That is where the ceremonial law comes in.

The ceremonial law (also called "the Law") was given to show how we as sinners can come back to God. It gave instructions about offerings, sacrifices, priests, mediation and things like that. It was a picture of the final One who would be our sacrificial lamb, our final priest, our mediator, our ultimate way to peace with God. So the ceremonial law was a picture, or shadow, of the cross. It was the answer to the broken moral law. You see, the ceremonial law was all about grace, the way of salvation. It pointed to the Lamb of God who takes away the sin of the world. The moral law reveals that we are sinners and separated from God. The ceremonial law showed man the way back to God. They are both together part of what God calls "The Law."

Now with that explanation let's look at some Scriptures. We see our sin and inadequacy in the moral law and it is that law that condemns us.

> "[19] Why, then, was the law given? It was given alongside the promise to show people their sins.
>
> [23] Before the way of faith in Christ was available to us, we were placed under guard by the law. We were kept in protective custody, so to speak, until the way

of faith was revealed. [24] Let me put it another way. The law was our guardian until Christ came; it protected us until we could be made right with God through faith. [25] And now that the way of faith has come, we no longer need the law as our guardian."
(Galatians 3:19,23-25)

"The Law was never meant to justify, the Law was meant to terrify." (John Stott)

"[20] For no one can ever be made right with God by doing what the law commands. The law simply shows us how sinful we are." (Romans 3:20)

"Mirror, mirror on the wall"

You remember the story of Snow White. The wicked queen of the land had a mirror that never lied. The moral law is like a mirror that reveals the truth about us. The Law is described in Scripture as a teacher given to expose our sin and lead us to faith in God.

Faith is the only way any man ever was, or ever can be, saved. But until man recognizes his sin and need he doesn't trust God. The moral law does just that. It condemns the sinner and reveals the totally bankrupt condition of our hearts. It drives us to Christ where we can find salvation.

Wet paint

Have you ever seen a sign that says, "Wet Paint"? What happened next? Come on, be honest. Yes, you put your finger in it didn't you? Before you saw that sign you were not even aware of the painted surface. The sign made you aware and then you took it from there and put your finger into the paint. Then you looked at the wet paint on your finger and realized how stupid that was. Did the sign make you do it? No. Does the Law make us sin? No, but without the Law we would not have a knowledge of sin. Once informed our fallen nature takes it from there. And afterwards we understand what we did.

> **"[To be sure] sin was in the world before ever the Law was given, but sin is not charged to men's account where there is no law [to transgress]."**
> (Amplified Bible, Romans 5:13)

> **"When we were controlled by our old nature, sinful desires were at work within us, and the law aroused these evil desires that produced a harvest of sinful deeds, resulting in death."** (Romans 7:5)

It is important that right after God gave the moral law (Exodus 20) he gave the ceremonial law (Exodus 25-40). Although these two functions of "the Law" may seem different they are part of God's one unchanging plan for man. First He shows man his need and then He provides the solution. It is common for people to talk about grace being a New Testament word or concept but the entire Law is actually about grace. It is God helping man see his true condition and then providing the way home for His wayward child. Now what do you call that? It is called grace. The Old Testament is about grace because it continually points the way to the Light. That is what "the Law" was all about, exposing and illuminating, guiding and leading to redemption.

Next chapter we will go further into this Law of Grace.

e you ever wondered?Have you eve
idered?Have you ever wondered?H
ever wondered?Have you ever wor
idered?Have you ever wondered?H
ever wondered?Have you ever wor
idered?Have you ever wondered?H

- Isn't the Old Testament about Law and the New Testament about Grace?

CHAPTER 7

The Law of Grace
THE WAY BACK TO GOD

I remember as a new Christian looking at those fascinating dispensational charts which were quite popular many years ago. There was that big word, "Law" which covered much of the Old Testament. And then the other big word, "Grace" covered the New Testament time line. The charts and drawings were very intriguing but, in my case, also very confusing. I had a hard time trying to make sense out of it. I knew that God never changed but the charts seemed to indicate that He did something one way and then did it a different way later. That confused me. That chart made me think that the Law had failed to save man, so therefore God instituted grace. That is the erroneous message I was left with as a new Christian. It took many years of Bible study to see that God indeed is God and has never changed. He has always had one unchanging plan and the entire Bible is about that one plan. There never was a plan "B."

> **"For I am the Lord, I do not change;**
> **that is why you, O sons of Jacob, are not consumed."**
> (Amplified version , Malachi 3:6)

No, God has not changed and neither has man. God is still loving and still holy. Man is still fallen and rebellious. God has always wanted His rebels to repent of their sins and come home. The Old Testament is a revelation of the Holiness of God, the sinfulness of man and the way home. The Old Testament is about Law and Grace. The New Testament is about the same things, Law and Grace.

Old Testament (concerning grace)

> **"but showing love to a thousand generations of those**
> **who love me and keep my commandments."**
> (Deuteronomy 5:10)

New Testament (Jesus speaking) (concerning law)

> **"Yes, ask me for anything in my name, and I will do it!**
> [15] **"If you love me, obey my commandments."**
> (John 14:14, 15)

The commandments were the same throughout all time, love God and love our neighbor as ourselves. God required it of man in the Old Testament and in the New Testament.

The New Testament tells an interesting story of a rich young man who thought he understood what the moral law meant. However, Jesus exposed his true heart.

> **"As Jesus started on his way, a man ran up to him and fell on his knees before him. "Good teacher," he asked, "what must I do to inherit eternal life?" [18]"Why do you call me good?" Jesus answered. "No one is good—except God alone. [19]You know the commandments: 'Do not murder, do not commit adultery, do not steal, do not give false testimony, do not defraud, honor your father and mother.'" [20]"Teacher," he declared, "all these I have kept since I was a boy." [21]Jesus looked at him and loved him. "One thing you lack," he said. "Go, sell everything you have and give to the poor, and you will have treasure in heaven. Then come, follow me." [22]At this the man's face fell. He went away sad, because he had great wealth."**

(Mark 10: 17-22)

The first thing we notice is that Jesus loved him. Jesus knew he was a lost sinner but loved him and helped him see the true meaning of the law. Why would Jesus tell him to sell everything and give it to the poor? That was not in the law, or was it? What is the law? Love God and love our neighbor. How do we love our neighbor? How do we love the poor? We should treat them like we would treat ourselves. Jesus told the man to do something that revealed what the moral law was really teaching. He was pointing out to the young ruler that if he loved his neighbor as he loved himself, then he would sell his things and give to his neighbor, the poor.

A true understanding of the meaning of the law exposed the young ruler's heart. It was selfish. He didn't want to share with his neighbor and therefore broke the second great commandment. Jesus also helped him see that his wealth had become a barrier in his relationship with God, which means he broke the first and great commandment. His sin was exposed.

The young man was deceived in thinking he had loved God and loved his neighbor as himself. When he understood the truth about the law and his own condition, he was sorrowful. That is the first step that leads to repentance. The young man had looked in the pure mirror of the law and did not like what he saw. Remember, the law was not meant to justify, it was meant to terrify. It was love that compelled Jesus to teach the man the moral law. The law exposed his true self, his sin, and was the only hope for the man to find eternal life. If he didn't understand his true sinful self he would eventually die deceived thinking he was righteous in himself.

Once the moral law has convicted us of our sin and lost condition then and only then are we ready for the remedy. The remedy is the cross where Jesus bore our sins and paid the eternal penalty we deserve. But before Jesus came to the earth how did those living in Old Testament times learn about God's remedy? That is where the ceremonial law comes in. The next section will show us how God revealed His one unchanging plan of redemption to those who lived before Jesus came, died and rose again. If I were to rename the Old Testament I would give it the title "The Way Home," by God. Grace literally drips out of the pages.

When Jonah cried out to God against the Ninevites, he said:

> **"Those who cling to worthless idols forfeit the grace that could be theirs."**
> (Jonah 2:8)

Jonah knew God wanted to redeem the people of Nineveh, the most wicked people on the earth. But Jonah hated the sinfulness of the people and had no interest in seeing them redeemed. He told the Lord they were forfeiting the grace God had for them. But God told Jonah to go and offer them another chance. God wanted them to know His grace but they needed to repent. So Jonah reluctantly took God's message to them and you know the rest of the story.

The prophet Isaiah also talked about how God offers grace to all men -

even the most wicked.

> **"Though grace is shown to the wicked, they do not learn righteousness; even in a land of uprightness they go on doing evil and regard not the majesty of the LORD."**
> (Isaiah 26:10)

The Law and the sheep dog

An interesting illustration of what the law does is found in the relation of sheep to the sheep dogs that drive them to a place of safety. That is what the moral law did. Without sheep dogs the sheep would ignorantly and blissfully roam the hills until they perish by wolves. The dogs use force and fear to drive the sheep to a place of protection with their shepherd. The book of Romans shows us that before the law we had no knowledge of sin or our real condition before God. The law exposes us for what we are. Once we get a good look at ourselves in God's mirror then terror enters in. We realize the danger we are in. We find ourselves lost and unable to rescue ourselves. Again, the law didn't justify but was meant to terrify. So that was a big purpose of the moral law, exposure. Once our guilt is exposed we are shut up to God, driven to the cross where there and there alone we find rescue. The law is what God uses to expose our need and drive us to the place of safety.

The real story is that God did not leave us helpless and condemned. Out of grace he gave the law to drive man to eternal life. In the Old Testament you will see this story in the shadows. There was light in the shadows. How bright was it? Let's just say you may need sunglasses.

The Law of Grace

SECTION 3

Camping in the Desert with God

Jesus is described in the book of Revelation as the "the Lamb that was slain from the creation of the world." Jesus' death and resurrection was in Creation's blueprints. God knew the cost of creation was the death of His son. Love made the call. Artists for centuries have painted depictions of Christ on the Cross. But had you lived in Old Testament times before Jesus Christ was born how would an artist have painted God's great plan of redemption? Here is what it would have looked like, a tent in the desert.

Whenever you read about the tabernacle and the temple in the Old Testament just remember you are looking at God's greatest visual aid about His great plan of salvation, His Son. The tabernacle in the wilderness is actually more than a picture; it is more like a complete photo album of Christ in the Old Testament times.

Exodus chapters 25-40 describe this amazing structure. A portable tent that went everywhere the children of Israel went. They packed it up and set it up and packed it up and carried it and set it up. This went on for 40 years until they finally carried it into the Promised Land. When the wandering of Israel had stopped and the dust settled the tabernacle was set up in Jerusalem. Later it was replaced with a larger and more permanent version of the same thing, the temple.

During the Exodus the tabernacle was the center of camp for 3.5 million people as they journeyed across the desert.

God actually gave Moses the blueprints for it. Since it was going to be the most important visual aid God would give to man to help him understand his fallen condition and his way back to God, it had to be built and operated exactly as God designed it. That is why there are so many details about its construction and operation. By specifying exact construction details God was protecting the message.

There is a tour leaving now to walk through God's campground. Would you like to join us?

e you ever wondered?Have you eve
ndered?Have you ever wondered?H
ever wondered?Have you ever wor
ndered?Have you ever wondered?H
ever wondered?Have you ever wor
ndered?Have you ever wondered?H

- Why are there so many details in the Old Testament about how things were to be constructed and how offerings were to be sacrificed?

CHAPTER 8

Blueprints for God's Dream Home

THE PLACE WHERE GOD AND MAN CAN LIVE TOGETHER

God cannot be contained in any building or man-made structure. That is clear in Scripture.

> **"The God who made the world and everything in it is the Lord of heaven and earth and does not live in temples built by hands."** (Acts 17:24)

Plans and a permit

So why would God instruct Moses to build a structure for Him, and actually give Moses the blueprints to make it, if God does not live in structures? Here is what He told Moses:

> **"Then have them make a sanctuary for me, and I will dwell among them. ⁹ Make this tabernacle and all its furnishings exactly like the pattern I will show you."**
> (Exodus 25:8)

It is important to note that God was not telling Moses He need- ed a physical place to live and if Moses would build the taber- nacle then God would come live there. No, what He was telling Moses was that when the tabernacle was constructed and the sacrificial system implemented then God and man could be brought back into relationship. With sin forgiven God could live with man. So, God was not telling Moses to build a place where He could live. He was telling Moses to build the tabernacle so that He could dwell with man.

Sin has caused us to be alienated from our Creator. Once sin is forgiven then we can be reconciled to our Creator and have the fellowship both He and we desire. The cross was the place where the sin of mankind was paid off. It is where the righteous demands of the Father were satisfied in His Son. It is where reconciliation was procured. The tabernacle in the Old Testament was a picture of the cross. It presented and provid- ed the benefits of the atoning work of Christ before He actually came and died for our sins. As a preview of the coming attrac- tion it pointed out many aspects of God's plan to redeem His fallen creation and restore His Kingdom reign.

Protecting the design

Since it was to be a picture of His Son, God was very clear and specific on how the tabernacle was to be built. He showed Mo- ses a detailed set of plans with the stamps and building per- mits all approved by the Great Architect Himself. He even told Moses what contractor to use so it would be done right.

"Then Moses said to the Israelites, "See, the LORD
has chosen Bezalel son of Uri, the son of Hur, of the
tribe of Judah, [31] and he has filled him with the Spirit
of God, with skill, ability and knowledge in all kinds
of crafts- [32] to make artistic designs for work in gold,
silver and bronze, [33] to cut and set stones, to work
in wood and to engage in all kinds of artistic crafts-
manship. [34] And he has given both him and Oholiab
son of Ahisamach, of the tribe of Dan, the ability to
teach others. [35] He has filled them with skill to do all
kinds of work as craftsmen, designers, embroiderers
in blue, purple and scarlet yarn and fine linen, and
weavers—all of them master craftsmen and designers." (Exodus 35:20-35)

The people all gave generously and the Bezalel Construction
Company built the tabernacle exactly like God wanted it built.
Bezalel was a master artist/craftsman. Isn't it interesting God
filled him with His Spirit to be an even better craftsman? God's
commands include His enabling power. It isn't only preachers
who have the anointing of God and filling of His Spirit. God is
the giver and sustainer for all who have chosen to follow Him.
By the way, Bezalel's name meant "In the shadow of God." That
is always a good place to be.

———————————

God was building His dream house, in a figurative sense, so He
wanted it built right. When it was completed and the sacrifices
were begun according to God's directives then God moved in
and traveled with His people across the desert.

The portable tabernacle in the desert was eventually

replaced with a permanent Temple when Israel stopped their wilderness wanderings and settled into the land God had promised. The same system of sacrifices and priests continued to point the way to salvation for many more generations until the day came when it was no longer needed. That was the day Jesus died on the cross.

The fine print

The blueprints of God were quite detailed and although each item is important, in this book I will focus only on the big items, the major elements. You are encouraged to go back and read the fine print. My goal is to give you the big picture so that the intricate details will make sense. I don't know about you but I have always enjoyed going to real estate open houses. Maybe it is curiosity about how others live. In the place my wife and I live it is getting quite common to see real estate tours. An entire afternoon is dedicated to visiting quality homes. The tour will go from one home to another and include a walk-through guided tour.

That is what we are going to do with the tabernacle. You can look in every room. The tour is ready to start; I can see the front door now.

e you ever wondered?Have you eve
idered?Have you ever wondered?H
ever wondered?Have you ever won
idered?Have you ever wondered?H
ever wondered?Have you ever won
idered?Have you ever wondered?H

- **What those living in the Old Testament times really understood about salvation?**

CHAPTER 9

God's Welcome Mat
AMAZING GRACE, HOW SWEET THE SOUND

Meeting God on His ground

If you want a strong argument in the Old Testament that it is a story of God's grace you only have to look at the gate of the tabernacle. God had given His people the Ten Commandments and they had broken them immediately. Israel had slapped God in the face (Actually we all have haven't we?) God could have commanded the earth to swallow them up. God could have rained down fire on them like he did the Egyptians. God could have stomped back up to Heaven and slammed the door so loud it shook the ends of the galaxy. God could have done anything he wanted with His rebellious kids. He is God.

So, what did God do? He gave Moses architectural plans for what He called the tabernacle and told him to build it and even specified the contractor to do the job. Once completed it was a clear picture of how the broken fellowship between man and

God could be restored. Now, what do we call that? Grace, grace, grace, grace. It was written all over the sands of the desert by the hand of God. God was saying, "I want you home." Anyone who thinks the Old Testament is only about law has not read it clearly. So Moses did what God said. He built this amazing tent and it became God's campground. When God decided to move He led the people across the desert with a cloud by day and a column of brilliant fire at night. When the cloud and fire stopped the camp was set up. When the cloud moved, the people followed and set up camp wherever and whenever God decided. God had made a way to dwell with His people and He was with them every step of the way.

The tabernacle was in the very center of the campground and continually spoke of the God of Grace, the God that wants to fellowship with man more than anything else. But the tabernacle also carried another message, namely the magnitude of sin and God's only solution to the problem.

Each part of the tabernacle visually communicated an aspect of God's great salvation plan. The tabernacle was a tent structure in a small courtyard. The courtyard was 150 feet long and 75 feet wide. It was enclosed by a continuous wall of white linen curtain. God was present in the midst of His people but He was also separated from them. The white curtain was a stark contrast with the animal skin tents of the people and the desert scenery. It represented the holiness of God. Man the sinner was outside and God, who is holy, was inside. This is where grace becomes very clear in the picture.

There was a door. A door. A way back to God!

It was the only part of the outer curtain that was not white but beautifully embroidered in four colors. It was God's welcome mat. In Japan, people decorate their home entrances to reflect who they are. They call it the "face of the house." That is what God did. His front door was a reflection of His face. It said, "Please come back, I want you home." He showed His face and it was beautiful.

The entire tabernacle is about Christ so we can look at each element and see Jesus in it. Since the gate is a picture of the eternal grace of God, we might expect it would teach us a lot about the one the Bible says was "full of grace and truth." Jesus said:

> **"I am the gate; whoever enters through me will be saved. "** (John 10:9)

God, the Divine Architect, designed the gate. Imagine what the people in the time of Moses saw when they approached the tabernacle. They had seen the power of God. They witnessed the drowning of Pharaoh's army and the awesome display of power on Mt. Sinai. They had seen Him in judgment and glory. They had been given the moral law on stone tablets and they had broken them. They knew they, like we, didn't deserve any favor from God. Yet He wanted them back.

As they approached the great white barrier with the cloud of God's glory hovering above the tabernacle like an overshadowing canopy there had to be a sense of fear and dread upon them. Then they came to the gate, that beautiful gate. It was different from the rest of the tent. It made them want to enter. Their fear turned from a paralyzing dread to a sense of worship and the type of fear of God that leads to forgiveness and peace.

> **"10 He does not treat us as our sins deserve or repay us according to our iniquities. 11 For as high as the heavens are above the earth, so great is his love for those who fear him;"** (Psalm 103:10,11)

Here are some of the impressions and lessons they learned when they approached the gate:

1. There was only one way into the presence of God.

The world may say that many roads lead to God but God says there is only one. Jesus is that only way. He is very clear about that."

> **"Jesus answered, "I am the way and the truth and the life. No one comes to the Father except through me."** (John 14:6)

2. The gate was wide.

The width of the outer curtain was 75 feet. The gate was 30 feet. God's arms were wide open. All who wanted to come could come. An old hymn chose words that would be well suited for the gate, "Though millions have come, there is still room for one; there is room at the cross for you."

3. The gate was attractive.

It could have been small, plain and hard to reach but no it was large, central and gorgeous. Grace abounded in the desert of sin. It was a beautiful thing. It radiated hope. The weariness of the journey, the burden of sin, and the weight of the guilt of sin all lifted when they approached the tabernacle. Hope was just beyond the gate.

4. The gate was accessible.

It was available to everyone all the time. No one was excluded, rich, poor, young or old. There were no hindrances to keep a person out. The only thing that kept a person out was himself. While writing this chapter one of our granddaughters was at our home. The little four year old came up to me while I was typing and said, "Grandpa, can you play with me?" I joked with her and said, "I am doing something very important, do you expect Grandpa to drop what he is doing and play with this little girl standing here?" I guess she saw the twinkle in my eye because she started to smile. I smiled, "Sure, let's play with the dolls and the doggie." The gate never closed. God loves nothing better than to stop what He is doing - running the universe - and spend time with his kids. He is always available. Even at night the pillar of fire broadcast the message far and wide that God was home and had left the night light on. He was available for anyone who wanted to visit. And He still is.

> **"By day the LORD went ahead of them in a pillar of cloud to guide them on their way and by night in a pillar of fire to give them light,"**
> (Exodus 13:21)

5. The gate was essential.

If anyone wanted to experience the forgiveness of God he had to go through that gate. Until then he remained lost in his sins no matter how religious he appeared or how good his intentions might be. There was no other way, no other pardon for sin. God never twisted a person's arm and made them go through but if they wanted forgiveness it was the only way.

> **"Salvation is found in no one else, for there is no other name under heaven given to men by which we must be saved."** (Acts 4:12)

6. The gate was the way to find mercy.

Grace and mercy are not the same, actually they are opposites. Grace is receiving something we don't deserve. Mercy is not getting what we do deserve.

> *"There's a widenesss in God's mercy,*
> *like the wideness of the sea*
> *There's a welcome for the sinner,*
> *and more graces for the good;*
> *There is mercy with the Savior; there is healing in his*
> *blood."* (Traditional Hymn)

When the dying, guilty and condemned thief on the cross next to Jesus looked at Him and said in a humble, repentant manner, "Lord, remember me," Jesus opened the gate of glory and beckoned him in.

> **"Mercy there was great and grace was free. Pardon there was multiplied to me. There my burdened soul found liberty, at Calvary."** (Hymn)

I hope you will never look at that gate again the same way. Once inside the courtyard the sinner was confronted with an awesome and horrible sight. Animals were being slaughtered. The sand was red with blood. A large brass object, the altar, was the central focus in the courtyard. It was a breathtaking sight.

ve you ever wondered?Have you eve
ndered?Have you ever wondered?H
ever wondered?Have you ever won
ndered?Have you ever wondered?H
ever wondered?Have you ever won
ndered?Have you ever wondered?H

- Why did God command people to sacrifice animals when we know in the New Testament that the blood of bulls and goats never did take away sin?

CHAPTER 10

Blood on the Doorstep

THE CROSS IN THE OLD TESTAMENT

We ate lunch one day at a barbecue restaurant and there was a sign on the door as we entered that said, "This is going to get messy!" That might have been an appropriate sign to put in the courtyard of the tabernacle near the bronze altar. These next two chapters are going to get messy.

Some call Christianity a bloody religion. There is no denying it. The death of Christ is at the center of God's incredible plan for the redemption of His fallen creation. "Without the shedding of blood there is no forgiveness of sins." Blood is central. Sin called for death. We are guilty. Jesus stepped up and said, "I will shed my blood in place of the sinner." So as we enter the tabernacle courtyard it should not be surprising that blood and death will be center stage.

When a person walked through the gate it was very clear what he saw. The bronze altar stood by itself with a roaring fire and the carcasses of sacrificial animals on the grate. Priests were attending the sacrifices and helping the other sinners who were slaughtering their sacrifices. It was a gruesome scene. It was designed to be.

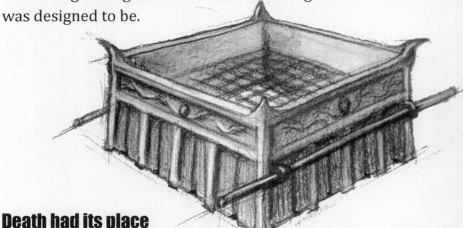

Death had its place

The word altar means "place of slaughter." Once the sacrifice was completed the pardoned sinner left the tabernacle. The priests took it from there. Man's part was to confess his sins and participate in the death of the animal. The message was loud and clear — the wages of sin is death.

Offerings could only be made at the bronze altar, nowhere else. Jesus died on the cross and offered himself on Calvary. Forgiveness is found nowhere else. Once the animal was killed and placed on the altar its blood was poured out at its base. Jesus, our final sacrifice, poured out His life onto the ground for you and me.

The Old Testament altar was God's

shadow of the final sacrifice, the Lamb that would one day come and become the final payment for all sin throughout all of time. Jesus was "the Lamb of God who takes away the sin of the world." Until that moment, when He died for our sins, the sacrificial system and the altar were a constant reminder to the people that salvation was by faith and that a substitute would take our place.

Altars - The true and the false

Who killed the first animal in recorded history? God did. When Adam sinned God killed an innocent animal and covered Adam and Eve with the bloody skin. The first altar was then built and animal sacrifices were established. Adam instructed his two sons, Cain and Abel, about the altar and the necessity of an animal's death when dealing with sin. Other offerings of thanksgiving and worship came later as God progressively revealed more about sacrifice and His Son. However, the shedding of blood was always necessary for forgiveness of sin. Man could not worship unless he first came through the blood.

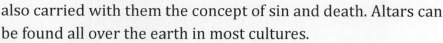

God's people always built altars. Those who chose not to follow God and wandered to different places on the earth also carried with them the concept of sin and death. Altars can be found all over the earth in most cultures.

Pagan civilizations built altars to the false gods they worshipped for the purpose of placating or appeasing them. The true system began in the Garden of Eden but counterfeits abounded over the earth from then on. Paul visited Athens in the first century and found altars there:

"He saw "an altar with the inscription, to the unknown God." (Acts 17:23)

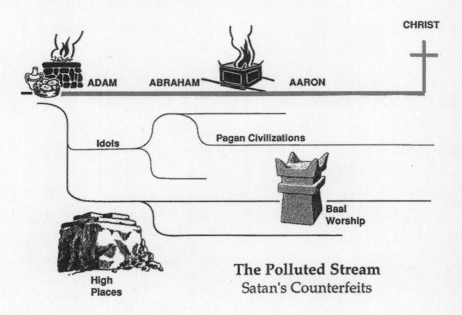

The Polluted Stream
Satan's Counterfeits

God's people built altars

Abel, Abraham, Isaac, Jacob and Elijah built altars. Noah built an altar before he built a house after the flood. When we get to Moses the ceremonial system has taken the place of individual altars. There was a formal priesthood and one high priest. The laws of the offerings were clearly revealed. The use of the altar is seen throughout all of human history from Adam to Calvary.

It always presented a message of sin, death and substitution of an innocent sacrifice.

The tabernacle had an altar, a large bronze one. When a sinner came in from the desert the wood fire was roaring and the sound of pain and squealing was everywhere as animals were being slaughtered. Priests in white garments were splattered in blood and the sand was red all around the killing stations and the altar. Blood ran down the bronze sides of the altar as priests with large bronze flesh hooks turned the carcasses and placed new ones on the large grate in the center of the altar. Death was in the air. No one questioned what the wages of sin were. One day God's pure Lamb would be placed on the altar of Calvary and bleed until He died. Listen and you can hear His last bleating, "It is finished." And with those words thousands of years and myriads of animal sacrifices came to an end. Their purpose was over. The shadow is finished.

Center stage

The bronze altar was Grand Central Station. Here the sinner, the priests and God all came together. God accepted the faith of the repentant sinner. The altar was central visually and it was central functionally. It was also vitally connected with other parts of the tabernacle. The blood shed there was carried into the Holy Place to be put on the Golden Altar and offered with prayer to God by the priest on behalf of the sinner. The hot coals taken from the bronze altar in the courtyard were the only coals that could be used to burn the incense in the Holy Place. Any other fire was called "strange fire" by God and was unauthorized. Aaron's sons Nadab and Abihu paid a severe penalty when they violated this instruction of God.

> **"But Nadab and Abihu died before the LORD when they offered strange fire before the LORD in the wilderness of Sinai; and they had no children."**
> (Numbers 3:4)

Why? Because sacrifice is the basis of forgiveness and a restored relationship with God. We can't go to God without the blood. Cain learned that lesson the hard way. Until we are forgiven we cannot worship.

The cross of Christ is the central moment in human history. Since the altar in the Old Testament sacrificial system was a picture of the cross it is clear why it occupied the central place in the courtyard of the tabernacle and was central to all the activities of the sinner, the priests and the sacrifices.

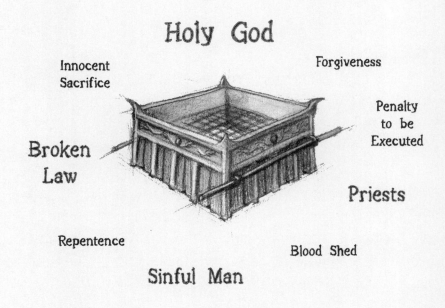

Holy God

Innocent Sacrifice

Forgiveness

Broken Law

Penalty to be Executed

Priests

Repentence

Blood Shed

Sinful Man

The sinner entered the tabernacle guilty and left pardoned. Justice was executed on the substitute. Judgment was accomplished. The consequence of sin was death and that had happened. By faith it was accomplished. God was satisfied. Seven chapters in Leviticus describe in great detail the five different types of sacrifices that were offered on the bronze altar. Now that you see what the altar was for and what it meant to those in that time, you will now better understand the five offerings.

That is the next chapter.

> **"In fact, according to the law of Moses, nearly everything was purified with blood. For without the shedding of blood, there is no forgiveness."**
> (Hebrews 9:22)

e you ever wondered?Have you eve
idered?Have you ever wondered?H
ever wondered?Have you ever won
idered?Have you ever wondered?H
ever wondered?Have you ever won
idered?Have you ever wondered?

**- Why some of the offerings
did not contain blood when we
know that without the shedding of blood there is no forgiveness of sin?**

CHAPTER 11

More than one way to skin a calf
THE FIVE OFFERINGS OF LEVITICUS 1-7

It was a time when killing was the law. Killing animals, that is. Have you ever personally watched an animal slaughtered? The first time I saw it was a shocking moment for me. No matter how many times you see it, blood is still a repulsive sight and often sickening. The smells, the sound, the entire scene is unsettling. God wanted man not only to see it but to actively participate in the death process. The sinner did the act, the priest assisted. Since the wages of sin is death, God made sure the sinner was the one responsible for the slaughter of the innocent victim.

Before man sinned there was no death on the earth. Death is only here because we are sinners and have brought the curse on ourselves. Until the day comes when God will finally remove death from the vocabulary of the universe, we have to live with it. We are not going to get out of here alive.

The five offerings described in Leviticus all took place on the great altar. They were the Burnt Offering, the Meal Offering, the Peace Offering, the Sin Offering and the Guilt Offering. God clearly separates them into two main categories. He calls the first three sweet savor offerings and last two non-sweet savor offerings.

The first three are described as a beautiful fragrance ascending to heaven. They were worship, thanksgiving and fellowship offerings all done by the one whose heart had been made right before God. The last two offerings were very different. There was nothing beautiful about them. They were a horror. They were the offerings for sins against God and against one's neighbor. With several million people trekking across the desert you can imagine that the bronze altar and the priests were quite busy. The fires never went out at the place of slaughter.

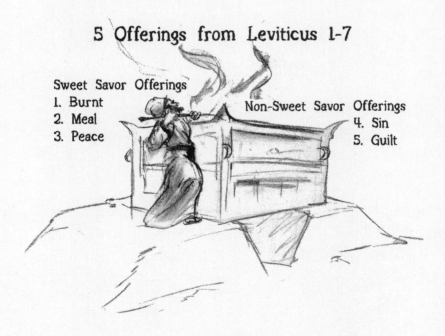

5 Offerings from Leviticus 1-7

Sweet Savor Offerings
1. Burnt
2. Meal
3. Peace

Non-Sweet Savor Offerings
4. Sin
5. Guilt

The five offerings are a detailed shadow of Christ's work on the cross. Let's look a bit deeper at each of the offerings. God gave a large number of details because He was talking about His Son and He had a lot to say.

1. THE WHOLE BURNT OFFERING (LEVITICUS CHAPTER ONE)

When offerings are first introduced in the Bible the burnt offering is the only one mentioned. It was used for both sin and worship. It gets its name primarily because the entire animal was consumed on the altar when it was offered to God.

> **"Then Noah built an altar to the LORD and, taking some of all the clean animals and clean birds, he sacrificed burnt offerings on it. [21] The LORD smelled the pleasing aroma . . ."**
> (Genesis 8:20, 21)

The Burnt Offering existed long before the time of Moses. Remember, the Levitical system (also called the Mosaic system) is the finished photograph. The details were less clear in the early pages of Scripture. But that never meant man did not have enough information to find peace with God. He certainly did.

By the time the tabernacle was constructed and the ceremonial law was complete, the Burnt Offering was designated as a worship offering. It was not used to deal with sin. It normally represented personal consecration and worship. It was completely voluntary like the other sweet savor offerings. The sin and Guilt Offering were mandatory. The Burnt Offering basically said to God, "I'm glad you are my Dad." The entire animal was consumed. Worship was complete. God loves it when we love Him.

It was a type of Christ who gave Himself fully, an offering acceptable to the Father. Burnt offerings were always a male without blemish and nothing was withheld - also part of the type of Christ who was male and without blemish, sinless.

> **"Be imitators of God, therefore, as dearly loved children and live a life of love, just as Christ loved us and gave himself up for us as a fragrant offering and sacrifice to God."** (Ephesians 5:2)

Today there are no more animal sacrifices. The shadows are over. Jesus fulfilled them all on the cross but we can still learn many lessons about our response to God.

> **"Therefore, I urge you, brothers, in view of God's mercy, to offer your bodies as living sacrifices, holy and pleasing to God - this is your spiritual act of worship."** (Romans 12:1)

2. THE MEAL OR GRAIN OFFERING (LEVITICUS CHAPTER TWO)

The second of the sweet savor offerings was the Grain Offering and contained no blood whatsoever. Grain was a common 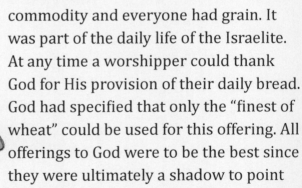 commodity and everyone had grain. It was part of the daily life of the Israelite. At any time a worshipper could thank God for His provision of their daily bread. God had specified that only the "finest of wheat" could be used for this offering. All offerings to God were to be the best since they were ultimately a shadow to point to Christ. Only the finest would do. Just as the animals were to be without blemish, the raw grain or baked unleavened cakes were also to be the very best. The offering always had to be without yeast or leaven. Leaven, or yeast, is a very useful additive to dough, but when it is used in the Bible as a symbol it frequently signifies corruption or evil. It spreads and permeates what it comes in contact with. So, since this offering had symbolism and was ultimately to be a type of Christ, God commanded it was to be unleavened. One thing you did find however with this offering was salt. This is a cultural issue. Salt was an eastern symbol of covenant relationship. In eastern cultures it was known as the salt covenant. Salt was always included in the meals associated with covenants. The meals became a strong bonding event between two parties.

> **"Whatever is set aside from the holy offerings the Israelites present to the LORD I give to you and your sons and daughters as your regular share. It is an everlasting covenant of salt before the LORD for both you and your offspring."** (Numbers 18:19)

Thus by using salt the worshippers of God were bound by solemn covenant to God. The main purpose of the Grain Offering was thanksgiving. It was an act of worship. It was not a sin offering. Until the sin and trespass offerings were first offered to God the Grain Offering had no value. A very familiar Biblical story tells of such a violation.

The Cain Mutiny

Understanding the Grain Offering helps us understand what happened in the story of Cain and Abel in Genesis four. Some people believe that God rejected

Cain because he presented an offering to God from the field, or from the work of his hands. And the argument is that nothing good can come from sinful hands, so God rejected the Grain Offering of Cain. That is actually not accurate. Both Cain and Able had equally noble professions. Cain was a farmer and Abel a herdsman. They both had valuable things to offer to God, grain and livestock. In the time of Moses both grain and livestock were not only acceptable worship offerings but both were commanded. There is nothing inherently wrong in either. They are both the work of the hands. Both are legitimate.

The issue in focus in the story of Cain and Abel was sin, not worship. Sin could only be dealt with by blood. God had made that clear to Adam and Eve when he killed the first animal. Once sin was forgiven then worship could take place. Cain came with a worship offering and Abel came with a sin offering. God did not respect the offering of Cain. He even told Cain that "Sin was at the door." Sin can only be dealt with by faith and through the blood. God did not respect Cain's offering because Cain did not respect God's way which ultimately pointed to Christ. It was in reality rejecting Christ. Had Cain offered a blood sacrifice first then his Grain Offering would have been gladly accepted by God.

Filling the pantry

The Grain Offering was not only a beautiful worship offering but it was also a very practical one. After a small memorial portion of the offering was mixed with olive oil and incense and burned on the bronze altar, the remainder of the offering was taken by the priests to be used for food. This was part of God's system to take care of those who did not farm or raise cattle but spent their days serving in the tabernacle. A parallel principle is found in the New Testament for pastors.

> **"In the same way, the Lord ordered that those who preach the Good News should be supported by those who benefit from it."** (1 Corinthians 9:14)

Honey was also forbidden along with leaven. Many scholars believe this was a specific warning against corrupting the pure offering with a pagan practice. For it was common in surrounding cultures to use honey in offerings to false gods. Jesus Christ is the Bread of Life. He was without sin, His character was flawless. Only an offering this pure could properly reflect the One it all pointed to.

3. THE PEACE OFFERING (LEVITICUS CHAPTER THREE)

The name of this offering was like a beautiful musical chord. Peace has been the illusive goal of peoples and nations since creation began. We can't seem to get along very well with others and the very thought of actually having peace with God is compelling. A familiar Christian song today proclaims "I am a friend of God." Isn't that a lofty thought and almost beyond our imagination that we can actually be God's friend? We can be at peace with the very God we have offended by our sin.

The Peace Offering was a wonderful thing to a people wandering the desert, living in tents and struggling to get along with each other. It is just as beautiful to us as well.

Like the first two offerings of Leviticus this was also a sweet savor offering, a voluntary act. This offering differed in that it focused on the inward parts of the animals being offered. Like the grain offering this offering also provided food for the priests. It was a time for fellowship and communion. The Peace Offering was taken from oxen, sheep and goats. Only the fat was offered on the altar and the rest was eaten as a fellowship meal with the priests, the worshippers' friends and God in the midst. It was like a barbeque dinner with friends and God was the guest of honor.

> *"This is indeed a vivid and graphic picture of communion; God Himself, His anointed priests, the offerer and his friends, all feasting together upon the same victim, the sacrifice of peace offering."*
> (H.A. Ironside, Lectures on Levitical Offerings)

This offering was like the beautiful promise found in 1 John 1:7

> **"But if we walk in the light, as he is in the light, we have fellowship with one another, and the blood of Jesus, his Son, purifies us from all sin."**
> (1 John 1:7)

The worshipper had previously been forgiven of sin and now celebrated reconciliation with his neighbor and his God in a great feast. Peace happens when reconciliation has taken place.

Family feud

In the year 2003 sixty members of two of the most notorious feuding families in America gathered in Pikeville, Kentucky and signed a truce ending the bloodshed of over 100 years of continual revenge. What began with a dispute over a pig eventually took a dozen lives. Then one day they sat down together and ended the madness. June 14 was declared by the governor of Kentucky as Hatfield and McCoy Reconciliation Day. Peace had finally come to the Kentucky Mountains.

The doctrine of reconciliation is seen in the Peace Offering. It was a time to examine oneself, a time of consecration and celebration. The inner parts of the animals were offered on the altar signifying self examination. Today's communion services in Christian churches encourage a similar time of introspection before sharing together in remembrance of the Lord's death. It is His death that makes our fellowship possible. The Peace Offering pointed to Christ our reconciliation, Christ our peace.

> **"For God was pleased to have all his fullness dwell in him, [20]and through him to reconcile to himself all things, whether things on earth or things in heaven, by making peace through his blood, shed on the cross. [21]Once you were alienated from God and were enemies in your minds because of your evil behavior. [22]But now he has reconciled you by Christ's physical body through death to present you holy in his sight, without blemish and free from accusation—"**
> (Colossians 1:19-22)

The first three offerings were optional, worship based and a sweet smelling fragrance to God. The next two are different.

The Sin and Guilt Offerings are not festivals and celebrations. They deal with the dark side.

4. THE SIN OFFERING (LEVITICUS CHAPTER FOUR)

The Psalmist wrote, **"Behold, I was shapen in iniquity; and in sin did my mother conceive me"**(Psalm 51:5 KJV). He was referring to fact that when Adam fell in the beginning, the human race fell because Adam was the human race. Since then all of his seed, and that includes us, are sons of Adam, born in sin. We have a sin nature. This is what the Sin Offering was about.

The Sin Offering was not primarily dealing with specific offenses against one's neighbor. That was handled with the fifth offering, the Guilt Offering. The Sin Offering was how the sinner agreed with God that he had a root problem, he was born in sin and his relationship with God was damaged.

In contrast the Guilt Offering was more focused on the specific damages done by sin to one's neighbor. The Sin Offering dealt with sin's root and the Guilt Offering with sin's fruit. The Sin Offering said "I am wrong." The Guilt Offering said, "I did wrong."

Even the high priest of Israel had to offer Sin Offerings for himself before he could offer the Sin Offering for the nation on the annual Day of Atonement. The only person ever born without the contamination of sin was the Lord Jesus Christ. That is why He was virgin born. The sinful seed of Adam was not in His DNA. Even Mary, his earthly mother, acknowledged her sinfulness when she went to the Temple and offered turtledoves as a Sin Offering.

> **"When the time of their purification according to the Law of Moses had been completed, Joseph and Mary took him to Jerusalem to present him to the Lord 23(as it is written in the Law of the Lord, "Every first-born male is to be consecrated to the Lord", 24and to offer a sacrifice in keeping with what is said in the Law of the Lord: 'a pair of doves or two young pigeons.'"** (Luke 2:22-24)

> **"If she cannot afford a lamb, she is to bring two doves or two young pigeons, one for a burnt offering and the other for a sin offering. In this way the priest will make atonement for her, and she will be clean."** (Leviticus 12:8)

There are many who believe Mary was sinless or immaculate but the Scripture is clear that she like the rest of us was born in sin and needed a Savior. That is why she later said:

> **"My soul glorifies the Lord 47and my spirit rejoices in God my Savior."** (Luke 1:46,47)

This is one of the primary differences in all world religions and Christianity. Many teach that man needs a teacher, a guru, a mentor. God says we need a Savior. We are not basically good, needing only to find that goodness or discover the spark of the divine within but we are desperate, fallen and depraved and need rescue. Even the free will God gave us is now a slave to sin. Scripture is very clear on this even if it sounds too negative to people.

> **"What shall we conclude then? Are we any better? Not at all! We have already made the charge that Jews**

and Gentiles alike are all under sin. [10]As it is written:
"There is no one righteous, not even one; [11]there is
no one who understands, no one who seeks God. [12]All
have turned away, they have together become
worthless; there is no one who does good, not even
one." (Romans 3:9-12)

The Sin Offering was how man agreed with God about his sinful condition and by faith found forgiveness and pardon. One clear distinction of the Sin Offering from all the other offerings was that after the inner parts were offered on the altar, the rest of the animal was taken outside of the courtyard to a place that was made ceremonially clean. There it was consumed on a simple wood fire. The Sin Offering dealt with the nature of sin. As an abomination to the holiness of God, it was taken out of His presence and consumed outside the camp.

Jesus was our Sin Offering. He paid for our sin, our sin nature. He fixed what was broken. He didn't die in the Temple on the great altar which was on the temple grounds but was taken outside the temple and died in a desolate place.

"We have an altar from which those who minister at
the tabernacle have no right to eat. [11]The high priest
carries the blood of animals into the Most Holy Place
as a sin offering, but the bodies are burned outside
the camp. [12]And so Jesus also suffered outside the city
gate to make the people holy through his own blood.
[13]Let us, then, go to him outside the camp, bearing the
disgrace he bore." (Hebrews 13:10-13)

"The next day John saw Jesus coming toward him and
said, "Look, the Lamb of God, who takes away the sin
of the world!" (John 1:29)

> **"God made him who had no sin to be sin for us, so that in him we might become the righteousness of God."** (2 Corinthians 5:21)

The New Testament makes a very clear statement about our sin nature and the Sin Offering.

> **"For what the law was powerless to do in that it was weakened by the sinful nature, God did by sending his own Son in the likeness of sinful man to be a sin offering. And so he condemned sin in sinful man"** (Romans 8:3)

The Old Testament sin offering was a clear shadow of Christ, God's Lamb, who came to die in our place as the final and only acceptable Sin Offering to God the Father.

5. THE TRESPASS (OR GUILT) OFFERING (LEVITICUS CHAPTERS FIVE AND SIX)

Besides the vertical issue of sin there was also the horizontal issue. Sin damages others. It violates the second great commandment to love our neighbor as ourselves.

As a non-sweet savor offering this one was also mandatory. Even though there is some overlap between the Sin and the Trespass Offering, this sacrifice focuses on the action of sin, not the principle of sin. Restitution is required in the trespass offering. The sinner would confess the sin, offer the animal and then make it right with his neighbor with an appropriate restitution. The Sin Offering was more about restoration of relationship with God whereas the Trespass Offering was restitution with neighbors. The Sin Offering was primarily in keeping with the first great commandment and the Guilt Offering with the second great commandment.

The Sin Offering served as a type of Christ who died for the "sin" of the world. The word "sin" a singular word. The Trespass Offering pointed to Christ who paid the penalty for our sins or acts (plural).

> **"Christ died for our sins, according to the scriptures"**
> (I Corinthians 15:3)

Jesus was our Sin Offering. Jesus was our Trespass Offering. Jesus was our Peace Offering, our Burnt Offering and our Grain Offering. Jesus paid it all. Like a fine diamond with its well-cut facets, the five offerings of Leviticus and the bronze altar reflect the light of God's salvation. When Jesus came to the earth it says of him "the people that walked in darkness have seen a great light."

Remember in an earlier chapter I said we would only be looking at the big pictures and not all the fine print, the small details? If you want to look at a passage that shows Christ in all the various offerings read the 53rd chapter of Isaiah. Watch for all the descriptions of sacrifice and offerings. 700 years before Christ was born the prophet understood that a Messiah who would come from God would be the One to fulfill the Levitical system. Isaiah saw the light in the shadows.

- Jesus our Burnt Offering - Fully acceptable to God.
- Jesus our Meal Offering - A perfect sacrifice without sin.
- Jesus our Peace Offering - Secured our peace with God.
- Jesus our Sin Offering - Paid the penalty for who we are, sinners by nature.
- Jesus our Guilt Offering - Paid for the damage we have done. We are sinners by practice.

At the altar the fire never went out. The priests never sat down. The work was never over until the day arrived when a humble carpenter hung on a Roman cross. There he poured out His pure blood onto the sand and bore the sin of the world. He absorbed the eternal wrath of God in our place. He died. God's holy demands were satisfied in the death of His Son. The shadow was finished. It led us to the cross as it was designed to do.

> **"Later, knowing that all was now completed, and so that the Scripture would be fulfilled, Jesus said, "I am thirsty." [29]A jar of wine vinegar was there, so they soaked a sponge in it, put the sponge on a stalk of the**

hyssop plant, and lifted it to Jesus' lips. [30]When he had received the drink, Jesus said, "It is finished." With that, he bowed his head and gave up his spirit."
(John 19:28-30)

Hallelujah, what a Savior!

If we stopped here it would be enough. If the tabernacle only contained the gate and the altar all men would have known enough to find eternal life. But there is more; the journey is not over. For the forgiven sinner he had gone as far as he could go into the tabernacle. From here on only the priests could go. It was as if there was a sign saying, "Authorized personnel only beyond this point." So before we continue our exploration of the rest of the tabernacle we need to take a look at the only ones authorized to go there. The next two chapters will introduce us to the priesthood that God established and why He did it.

Let's go meet the men in white.

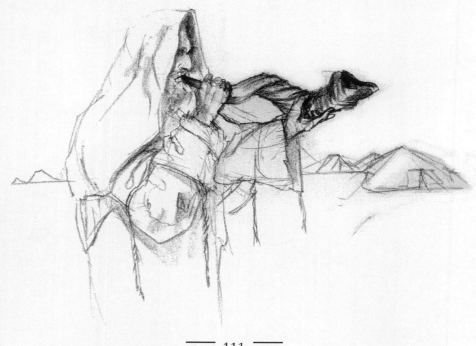

SECTION 4

Priests - when you need a middle man

There is the story of a peasant man dying in the hospital. He was a simple Christian believer. One day the local Catholic chaplain dropped in for a visit. The dying man said, "Yes, what do you want? The priest said he was visiting the sick and could forgive the man's sins if he wished. "Let me hold your hands" the dying man said to the priest. The priest gently reached out to take the sick man's wrinkled hands. The peasant examined the hands of the priest and then exclaimed, "You are an imposter!" Startled, the priest stepped back, "Why would you say that?" "Because," the dying man responded, "the One who forgives my sins has nail holes in hHis hands!"

That story illustrates the wide range of belief on the topic of the priesthood. Anywhere in the world you travel you will see priests of all variety. Within the general Christian umbrella the concept of the priesthood is found in Roman Catholicism, Episcopalian, Anglican, Orthodox and Mormonism. Most major religions have them. Hinduism, Buddhism, tribal animists and the occult all have their own priestly hierarchy. I once met a man who claimed to be high priest of the temple of the sun god, Ra. Priests or ministers who have priestly duties are found everywhere and people have many different beliefs about them.

The univesal messsage of priests

Having traveled extensively on five continents for the past 35 years I can attest that priesthood is universal. Even those in primitive cultures know inwardly that there is a Creator and that they have offended Him. In one way or another, they seek the help of a holy man to act on their behalf to satisfy the wrath of the offended deity. From the jungles of Borneo to the cathedrals of Europe that same belief can be found in various forms.

It is a confusing issue to many as well as an emotional one. One of the big problems is that God clearly instituted the Levitical priesthood. Priests in the Bible were not man's idea but God's appointed office. So, why all the confusion? Do God's priests still exist and function? Many say yes and others say no. Does the Scripture speak to this issue? The answer is yes. Then we must listen to God no matter what man says.

Let's go back and look at priests the way God instituted them and answer the question, "Is the office of priest still with us today." If it is then what should it look like? If it isn't then the priests of today are man's attempt to duplicate in the flesh what God instituted in the Spirit. If priests do exist today in

God's plan then many priests in the world are counterfeit. They can't all be authentic since they often contradict each other. It is a big subject but fortunately we have light. And once again, that light is found in the shadows.

ve you ever wondered?Have you eve
idered?Have you ever wondered?H
ever wondered?Have you ever won
idered?Have you ever wondered?H
ever wondered?Have you ever won
idered?**Have you ever wondered?**H

- What is the purpose of a priest?

- Don't we have direct access to God without going through a human mediator?

-Why do priests dress differently than other people?

CHAPTER 12

Levi Genes

MEN IN WHITE

It is very important to understand that the complete Levitical system was exactly that, a system. It contained many components that together constituted the shadow of the cross. It must be seen and left intact as a system the way God designed it. Together it taught man about God's one unchanging plan of redemption for His creation. We can't take any one element out and still have the same message. All of it is important for the overall picture.

Remember, God sent a picture before He sent the person. The tabernacle, priests, sacrifices, structures, feasts and the priests made up the picture. No part stands on its own. And when Jesus said it was finished He meant the entire system, all of it, not just parts of it. It was all a shadow that ended at the foot of the cross. It accomplished its purpose and then it was over. All of it. The animal sacrifices were finished. The tabernacle and all its parts were finished. The priests were finished. There are groups today that still have priests in their church or religion. If they choose to do that then they also need to have all the parts. It is all or nothing. It was an inseparable system. If a person is going to have priests then they should also have animal sacrifices. After all, that is what the priests did. That would include all the ceremonies and a bronze altar. They would also need to follow the laws of the offerings. But if all these were a shadow of the good things to come then when Jesus came, died and resurrected, He fulfilled the entire system. It is all over. The picture is gone. The Lord has come.

Now we need to pay a visit to the Levites in order to see some of the great lessons God taught His people through this fascinating office of the priesthood.

Who were the Priests?

1. Early Priests
In the early pages of the Bible every man was in essence his own priest. There was no formal priesthood for centuries. Even after animal sacrifices and burnt offerings were well understood there was no formal priesthood. People made stone altars and offered burnt offerings for both sin and worship. This continued from Adam to Abraham. Abraham met Melchizadek who was both a king and a priest of Salem. But Abraham, without the assistance of a priest, took Isaac to Moriah to offer his son in obedience to God.

The office of the priest was established in detail by God in the time of Moses. There were other priests in the various cultures by then but Gods' system was not completely revealed. Even Jethro, Moses' father in law, was a priest in Midian. Holy men were chosen in different cultures to represent the people before their deities. When God formally established the Levitical priesthood in the time of Moses the picture He had planned was complete.

2. The Levites

Just as with other parts of the tabernacle the priests are described in detail. And for the same reason. God protected the design and thus protected His message which was the picture of His Son. Of the twelve tribes of Jacob, God chose one who would become a servant tribe. That was the tribe of Levi. Like a large stage crew, the Levites set the tabernacle up and tore it down whenever it moved. Levi had three sons and each of these sons and their family lines were given specific duties. One of the sons, Kohath, was a steward of the most holy items.

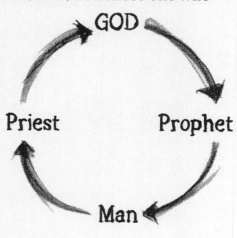

Moses and his brother, Aaron, were Koathites. Aaron was chosen by God to be the first High Priest of Israel. Moses was the Prophet of God. Remember this drawing?

The sons of Aaron were designated to be the priests. Only sons of Aaron could be priests. Even if a person wanted to become a priest he could not. He had to be born into Aaron's line.

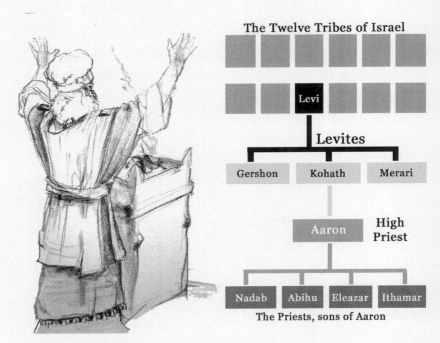

The Twelve Tribes of Israel

Levi

Levites

| Gershon | Kohath | Merari |

Aaron — High Priest

| Nadab | Abihu | Eleazar | Ithamar |

The Priests, sons of Aaron

This diagram shows how it worked.

The Levites were responsible for the physical structure of the tabernacle. They were also responsible for the spiritual needs of the people. Mostly the priests assisted the people in the sacrifices. Ultimately they were mediators between a holy God and sinful man.

The priests had a vital role in God's two-fold program of Redemption and Kingdom. The priests were the divinely appointed people He used to administer His program of redemption. They were custodians of the ceremonial law assigned to help the sinner find his way back to God.

Moses, on the other hand, was the prophet, the mouthpiece

or spokesman for God, sent to deliver the moral law to the people. He was an ambassador of the Kingdom of God. He presented the holiness and demands of God to the people. Moses was the law giver and Aaron was the grace giver.

The entire system was like a play called "The Messiah." The Levites helped paint the set and fix up the building, the sons of Aaron were the stage crew and the High Priest was the best supporting actor. The leading man was a lamb. We were the villain and killed the leading man. The play ran for 1,400 years then held its final performance the night Jesus was in the audience. Some tried to get the actors to do encore performances but the Romans tore down the theatre in AD 70.

Details, Details, Details

The most important thing to keep in mind when reading all the laws and details concerning the priests is the big picture. Don't get bogged down in the small print. It all will make sense if you keep the overall purpose of God in mind. At first it can be overwhelming - the clothing, the duties, the precise rituals, etc. God wanted to make sure that the message was clear for generations to come so he gave precise instructions. He was painting a picture of His son and He didn't want the portrait to turn into a wild piece of modern art. He made sure they colored within the lines for this one.

Here is a simple summary of some of the main points of the Levitical priesthood:

- A priest began his service at age 30. That is why Jesus, our Great High Priest, didn't start His earthly ministry until age 30.

- Their garment was a simple white linen coat. It was to symbolize purity. God is holy and He demanded that those who serve would have clean hands and a pure heart.

- Their main role was mediatorial. They were God's middle men.

- Substitution was two-fold. The slain animal was a substitute for the judgment the sinner deserved and the sinner had access to God in the person of the priest.

- All the 11 other tribes received a land inheritance in the Promised Land. Levi did not. The Lord was their inheritance.

- The bronze laver was used only by the priests. It was located at the entrance of the tabernacle building just past the bronze altar. It was forged from the mirrors of the women. God expected a priest to examine and cleanse himself before he entered the Holy Place.

And lastly, and possibly the most important issue and one of the primary themes of the book of Hebrews:

- The priesthood had an expiration date: the cross of Christ.

Any formal priesthood in any religion today is simply a man-made attempt to resurrect or reconstruct something that was finished at Calvary. Actually, after Calvary, the only mention of priests in Scripture refers to all believers as a kingdom of priests. We will find out why in chapter 14.

Yes, the formal priesthood was part of the shadow and was finished along with all the other parts of the Levitical system. It didn't fail any more than the law failed. None of it was ever meant to make a man right with God. Man found eternal life by grace through faith back then just as he does today. The Law, the priests and the sacrifices all revealed to man his inadequacy before God. The Levitical system was a vivid illustration of his true fallen state. It was God's sheep dog to drive him into the safety of the sheepfold.

Building a Custom Home

Suppose you want to build a custom home for yourself. You would find a builder and an architect to draw up your plans. He would supply you with a realistic rendering of your future house. For the next six months you would eagerly await the completion of your new home. In the meantime, you would show your friends the picture you have of the house that is under construction.

But then one day the wait is over. The builder calls you and says, "It is finished." You call all your friends and family and meet at the new house. When you all arrive there what are you going to do? Will you gather around the blueprints and discuss them or are you going to go inside the finished house and look around. Of course you will go into your new home. Why would you sit around and discuss the picture when you finally have the real thing? The house is finished. You no longer need the drawing. It was just a picture to show you what was coming. "It is finished!"

Before we leave the subject of the priesthood we need to look at the one priest that was different from all the others. Then we will examine what it means to us today.

e you ever wondered?Have you eve
ndered?Have you ever wondered?H
ever wondered?Have you ever won
ndered?Have you ever wondered?H
ever wondered?Have you ever won
ndered?Have you ever wondered?H

- What is Jesus doing today? He became a man and died for our sins. He is coming again but what is He doing now?

CHAPTER 13

God's Wardrobe
HEAVEN'S FASHION SHOW

There were thousands of priests but only one high priest. Aaron was God's first appointed high priest and his sons and their lines were the priests. The only way for a person to become a priest was to be born a priest.

The New Testament is abundantly clear that the high priest of the Levitical system was a type, or picture, of our Lord Jesus Christ. Jesus, in His resurrected body, is our Great High Priest. But without the Old Testament, we would have no idea what that meant.

> "Therefore, since we have a great high priest who
> has gone through the heavens, Jesus the Son of God,
> let us hold firmly to the faith we profess. [15]For we do
> not have a high priest who is unable to sympathize
> with our weaknesses, but we have one who has been

tempted in every way, just as we are—yet was without sin. [16]Let us then approach the throne of grace with confidence, so that we may receive mercy and find grace to help us in our time of need."
(Hebrews 4:14-16)

Aaron was the first high priest of the nation. God designed the garments he wore. They were absolutely stunning in appearance and workmanship. When the Scripture speaks of the texture, quality, or workmanship of the material, it is always the best: fine linen, pure gold, precious stones and costly ointment. Nothing but the best could point to the Perfect One, the Lord Jesus Christ. Some say clothes make the man. In this case clothing pictured the man.

The clothing of the high priest of Israel gives us a beautiful picture of the character and attributes of Jesus, our Great High Priest. Then when we look at the duties and activities of Israel's high priest we understand the role of our greater High Priest. The high priest was clearly the central figure in Israel. Christ is the central figure in all creation. A high priest, like other priests could not begin his public ministry until age 30. We mentioned in the previous chapter that Jesus according to the ceremonial law had to wait until He was 30 to begin His public ministry since He is our Great High Priest.

God's Clothing Business

The first garments in the Bible were fashioned from animal skin, probably lamb, by God for Adam and Eve. They had covered themselves with fig leaves after the Fall. God communicat-

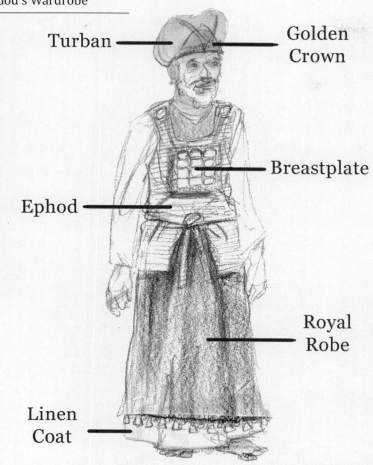

Turban — Golden Crown

Breastplate

Ephod —

Royal Robe

Linen Coat —

ed from the very beginning that only the blood of an innocent substitute could cover sin. God also designed the garments of the high priest. Just as we saw with the first couple, clothing has a message when God is the fashion designer. Much detail is given concerning the high priest's garments because God had so much to teach man about who He is and what He was about to do. The garments will be dealt with in the order in which the high priest would have put them on. Just as we handled the other parts of the tabernacle we will only note the major garments and details and not get bogged down with the minor points.

1. The White Linen Coat

This was the only garment common to both priests and the high priest. For the high priest it was his undergarment. But for the priests it was their only garment. The white coat pictured purity, holiness and righteousness. It was made from "fine linen" which pictured the nature of the office then and ultimately the sinless nature of Christ.

> **"May your priests be clothed with righteousness"**
> (Psalm 132:9)

2. The Blue Robe, or the Robe of the Ephod

The white linen coat was a covering, The robe was royal apparel. Blue was a symbol of kingly dignity. When Christ was crucified the jeering soldiers mocked his claim of being King of the Jews by putting a robe on him.

> **"Then the governor's soldiers took Jesus into the Praetorium and gathered the whole company of soldiers around him. [28]They stripped him and put a scarlet robe on him, [29]and then twisted together a crown of thorns and set it on his head. They put a staff in his right hand and knelt in front of him and mocked him. "Hail, king of the Jews!" they said."**
> (Matt. 27:27-29)

There is an interesting description in Revelation of Christ's return as King of Kings. He is wearing a robe once again, this time dipped in blood. And His army is an army of priests, clothed in white garments.

> **"I saw heaven standing open and there before me was**

a white horse, whose rider is called Faithful and True. With justice he judges and makes war. ¹²His eyes are like blazing fire, and on his head are many crowns. He has a name written on him that no one knows but he himself. ¹³He is dressed in a robe dipped in blood, and his name is the Word of God. ¹⁴The armies of heaven were following him, riding on white horses and dressed in fine linen, white and clean. ¹⁵Out of

his mouth comes a sharp sword with which to strike down the nations. "He will rule them with an iron scepter." He treads the winepress of the fury of the wrath of God Almighty. ¹⁶On his robe and on his thigh he has this name written: KING OF KINGS AND LORD OF LORDS."

(Revelation 19:11-16)

At the base of the royal coat of the high priest was a hem of ornaments, golden bells and woven pomegranates. It had a beautiful ring as the High Priest walked among the people. Pomegranates were a fruit of the promised land and the bells were a sign of life. When they heard the sound of the bells they were reminded that they had a living mediator between themselves and God. It was the music of hope.

"but because Jesus lives forever, he has a permanent priesthood. ²⁵Therefore he is able to save completely those who come to God through him, because he always lives to intercede for them." (Hebrews 7:24, 25)

3. The Ephod

The ephod was an apron-like garment. It had a front piece and back section and hung over the shoulders. It was tied at the waist with a belt or sash. The thread colors were blue, purple, scarlet and white. The whole unit was held firmly on the high priest by the waistband. Actual gold was beaten into thin plates, then cut into strips and woven into the ephod. It was an object of great brilliance and beauty. The front and back panels were connected by shoulder pads with inset onyx stones engraved with the names of the twelve tribes of Israel. The ephod served primarily as a base for the breastplate. But the word "ephod" itself became synonymous with authority and determining the will of God.

> **"They mounted the onyx stones in gold filigree settings and engraved them like a seal with the names of the sons of Israel."** (Exodus 39:6)

Whenever the high priest went into the presence of God he symbolically bore the tribes of Israel on his shoulders. It communicated to the people then that they had a sufficient mediator. And it ultimately pointed to our glorious Great High Priest who knows and intercedes for his children.

4. The Breastplate

It was sometimes called the breastplate of decision making. The breastplate was a one foot square embroidered pouch that hung on the ephod. There were twelve precious stones set into the front of the breastplate, each with the name of a different tribe of Israel. The stones were all different and brilliant. It pictured the unity and diversity of the nation. Inside the pouch of the folded over breastplate were two precious stones known as the Urim and Thummim. God used these stones to reveal His will to His people through the high priest. It is unknown today just how this was done. Many elaborate theories exist but the Scripture is silent on how this was accomplished or exactly why God chose this way of revealing His will to His people through the high priest.

The high priest carried the names of the tribes over his heart as he approached God. It serves as a picture of our Great High Priest who knows His sheep and keeps them near His heart at all times. For the children of Israel they heard the sound of the bells, saw the beauty of the garments and knew their names were borne on the high priest shoulders and carried near his heart. They were assured they had a mediator who lived and carried their needs before the presence of God. They had an advocate who was just like them but who had direct access to God to plead their case.

> **"But because Jesus lives forever, his priesthood lasts forever. [25] Therefore he is able, once and forever, to save those who come to God through him. He lives forever to intercede with God on their behalf. [26] He is the kind of high priest we need because he is holy and blameless, unstained by sin. He has been set apart from sinners and has been given the highest place of honor in heaven. [27] Unlike those other high priests, he does not need to offer sacrifices every day. They did this for their own sins first and then for the sins of the people. But Jesus did this once for all when he**

offered himself as the sacrifice for the people's sins."
(Hebrews 7:24-27)

5. The Turban

A middle Eastern style turban was fashioned with cloth strips onto the head of the high priest. It pictured wisdom of their spiritual leader.

6. The Gold Crown

Whenever the forehead is described in Scripture and used as a symbol it represents the thoughts of a person or his total character. Listen to what God said to the Prophet Ezekiel:

> **Ezekiel 3:9**
> **I will make your forehead like the hardest stone, harder than flint. Do not be afraid of them or terrified by them, though they are a rebellious house."**

God used the word "forehead" to represent the nature of the person or group he was talking about. He was telling Ezekiel the people of Israel were a stubborn people and God would give Ezekiel stubbornness to match in his call to relentless faithfulness in preaching. Or, when God referred to a people as having a harlot's forehead (Jeremiah 3:3) He meant they were an unfaithful people.

So when God designed the garments for the high priest He included a golden crown to be placed on his forehead with the words, "Holiness unto the

Lord" engraved on it. The office of high priest was a holy office, set apart to serve a God who is holy. It ultimately represented Jesus Christ and His holiness.

- **The garments** all pictured the character of the office of the high priest of Israel and ultimately were a shadow that directed us to our Great High Priest.

- **The duties and activities** of Israel's high priest help us understand what Jesus is doing today.

The Work of the High Priest

Aside from being a spiritual figurehead and providing hope and security for the nation, the high priest basically had two roles. First, He offered sacrifices for the nation. He alone went into the Most Holy Place on the Day of Atonement to mediate between the nation and God. Second, he made intercession for sin. So the high priest was involved in atonement and intercession. Jesus came as a sacrifice and is coming again as a reigning king. He came to pay the price for redemption and to establish His Kingdom.

Today He is our Great High Priest who ever lives to make intercession for us. He bears our name on his shoulders and carries us near His heart as He acts as our advocate and mediator before the Father.

An interesting observation is that there were no provisions to sit down in the tabernacle. No chairs. Why? The work was never done. Sin was always present among the people so the work of the priest and the high priest never ended. But when

Jesus died for our sins and rose again the Scripture says "He sat down." It was finished.

> **"In the past God spoke to our forefathers through the prophets at many times and in various ways, [2]but in these last days he has spoken to us by his Son, whom he appointed heir of all things, and through whom he made the universe. [3]The Son is the radiance of God's glory and the exact representation of his being, sustaining all things by his powerful word. After he had provided purification for sins, he sat down at the right hand of the Majesty in heaven."**
> (Hebrews 1:1-3)

The fires on the altars have now gone out, the smoke no longer rises. The atoning sacrifices which prefigured His final atoning sacrifice are no longer needed. He sat down. Salvation is a gift. It is received by grace through faith, not by anything we can do. He did it all and sat down. The work of the atonement is over, but today, as our Great High Priest, His intercessory role is not over.

———

Here is something to think about. If Jesus Christ is our Great High Priest and we are His children, born of God, then that makes us children of the high priest. What were children of the high priest called in the Levitical system? That's right, priests. All who are born again would be priests. Does the New Testament support this? That is what the next chapter is about.

e you ever wondered?Have you eve
ndered?Have you ever wondered?H
ever wondered?Have you ever won
idered?Have you ever wondered?H
ever wondered?Have you ever won
idered?
Have you ever wondered?

- What do the priests in the Old Testament have to do with us today?

CHAPTER 14

Birth Right

ARE THERE PRIESTS TODAY?

Before we return to the tabernacle tent and enter the Holy Place and the Holy of Holies we need to look at something important. We have established that God's reason for the priesthood in the Old Testament was to show man that he needed help in order to come into relationship with God. Sin had forged an impenetrable barrier between God and man. Nothing man could do could satisfy the holy and just demands of God.

Man in his fallen condition was not able to find his way back. He needed help. So God paid a penalty He did not owe so we, who were incapable of paying for what we did owe, could be forgiven of our debt. God paid the debt in full. He established the ceremonial law with its sacrifices and priests in order to help man understand his need for, and way to, God. When Jesus paid the final sacrifice the purpose of the ceremonial law was over. The sacrifices and priests which pointed to the work of

Christ on the cross were finished. Today we don't need animal sacrifices; we have Christ the Lamb of God. And we don't need human mediators because we have Christ our Great High Priest.

But just as Jesus continues on in the role of Great High Priest there is an interesting new relationship all true believers have with him. We, as his children, are actually priests. Only sons of Aaron could be priests in the Old Testament. Today, sons of our final Great High Priest take over the privileges and responsibilities pictured in the Old Testament priesthood. They were born priests. So are we. All who trust Christ as Savior are born again into a new and royal priesthood. No, there are no animals to sacrifice but there is a great and wonderful set of roles we have been given. The only references in the New Testament to priests after the resurrection of Christ are to all believers. This doctrine is known as the priesthood of the believer.

> "... you also, like living stones, are being built into a spiritual house to be a holy priesthood, offering spiritual sacrifices acceptable to God through Jesus Christ. [9]But you are a chosen people, a royal priesthood, a holy nation, a people belonging to God, that you may declare the praises of him who called you out of darkness into his wonderful light."
> (1 Peter 2:5, 9)

> "Grace and peace to you from him who is, and who was, and who is to come, and from the seven spirits before his throne, [5]and from Jesus Christ, who is the faithful witness, the firstborn from the dead, and the ruler of the kings of the earth. To him who loves us and has freed us from our sins by his blood, [6]and has

made us to be a kingdom and priests to serve his God and Father—to him be glory and power for ever and ever! Amen." (Revelation 1:5, 6)

Since God refers to all believers as priests what does that mean? We know it does not mean we are to sacrifice animals. God would not have used that designation if it wasn't for a purpose. So let's briefly look at the principles from the Old Testament that apply to us today.

1. Sons of the Great High Priest

As we mentioned an Old Testament priest had to be born a priest. There was no other way to be a priest. They had to be a son of the high priest. When we are born again we become children of the Great High Priest and, therefore, we become priests automatically. It has nothing to do with education, training or ordination. It is only by birth that one enters into the priestly family.

> **"But to all who believed him and accepted him, he gave the right to become children of God. [13] They are reborn—not with a physical birth resulting from human passion or plan, but a birth that comes from God."** (NLT, John 1:12.13)

In the Old Testament if a person was not a son of the high priest there was nothing he could do to become a priest. Today we all have the great privilege of trusting Christ as Savior and High Priest. We can all become part of the kingdom of priests God talks about.

2. Duty Bound

Just as the Old Testament priests had certain duties we also share similar duties.

We, like the priests of old, are stewards of the things of God and guardians of His word.
We are to care for His household. Remember, He is coming for His stuff. They were servants of others. The priests served the people 24/7. Jesus said the greatest in the Kingdom of God was servant of all. As priests we are called to serve. They were available at all times, not just when it was convenient.

They had a mediatorial role.
This one can be wrongly understood today. God had always provided a way for man to find forgiveness and eternal life. The priests had a role in that. They assisted the lost and the worshiper alike. They helped man understand and facilitated the process. We need to live lives and share a message that shows man the way to find peace with God. We are to serve the body and love one another. It is that love that will show the world, according to Jesus, that we are genuine. Our lives should draw men to the Savior in all we do and say. We are still the mediatorial link to God for the unbeliever. They watch us. They need the message we have. They need the hope we have. Paul describes the proclamation of the gospel as a priestly duty for all believers.

> "... to be a minister of Christ Jesus to the Gentiles with the priestly duty of proclaiming the gospel of God, so that the Gentiles might become an offering acceptable to God, sanctified by the Holy Spirit."
>
> (Romans 15:16)

One of the primary roles of the priests was that of intercessor. We will look at this further when we get to the Golden Altar inside the Holy Place in the next chapter. It was at this altar that prayer was made on behalf of the people. We too, as a kingdom of priests, are called to be intercessors. Prayer connects us and them with God. Priests stand in the gap. It is a priestly duty.

3. Cleaned and Dressed up

Priests had a preparation they had to go through to meet God. They put on all white garments. The garments spoke of God's call for personal holiness. This is almost a strange concept today with our casual approach to worship and prayer. I am not suggesting that special clothing or rituals are needed for the believer. But we must not lose sight that our God is a holy God and He wants His people to live lives that honor Him.

Not only did the priests put on all white but they had to be

cleansed at the bronze laver at the entrance of the tent of meeting. The priests would wash their hands and feet and examine themselves before they entered the holy place. This was yet another visual reminder that entering the presence of God was not to be taken lightly.

> "Who may ascend the hill of the LORD? Who may
> stand in his holy place? He who has clean hands and a
> pure heart, who does not lift up his soul to an idol or
> swear by what is false."
> (Psalm 24:3, 4)

The high priest initially clothed the priests when they became priests and in essence that is what our Great High Priest does for us. We stand today forgiven and justified by faith. Our righteousness is "imputed" or put onto us by our Great High Priest. But we are still responsible to walk in a manner worthy of that calling. The theological term for this is sanctification. We are set apart for God's special work.

When a priest entered into active service he had a bath, a full cleansing. After that he only washed his hands and feet at the laver before he entered the Holy Place. This image is picked up in the New Testament for all believers.

> "And that is what some of you were. But you were
> washed, you were sanctified, you were justified in the
> name of the Lord Jesus Christ and by the Spirit of our
> God." (1 Corinthians 6:11)

> "Jesus answered, "A person who has had a bath needs
> only to wash his feet; his whole body is clean. And
> you are clean, though not every one of you." 11For he
> knew who was going to betray him, and that was why
> he said not every one was clean." (John 13:10, 11)

It was a beautiful picture of what happens at salvation and it describes what our walk of faith should look like.

4. The Privileged Few

Not everyone was a priest. So it is today. Many are called, Jesus said, but few are chosen. The way of destruction is a path many take but the way to life is traveled by a few. To be a child of God is an incredible privilege. And just think, as priests we have unhindered access to God at any time.

> "Therefore, since we have a great high priest who has gone through the heavens, Jesus the Son of God, let us hold firmly to the faith we profess. [15]For we do not have a high priest who is unable to sympathize with our weaknesses, but we have one who has been tempted in every way, just as we are—yet was without sin. [16]Let us then approach the throne of grace with confidence, so that we may receive mercy and find grace to help us in our time of need. - those outside the priesthood (unbelievers) don't have this privilege" (Hebrews 4:14-16)

The priests of the Old Testament were custodians and defenders of the Word of God. They were called to follow it and lead others to the truth and salvation. Many in the world today still have no access to the word of God. When is the last time you thanked God for these amazing priestly privileges?

5. A Pilgrim Lifestyle

When God divided up the Promised Land into parcels He gave each tribe a portion of the land. Each tribe, that is, except Levi.

> "At that time the LORD set apart the tribe of Levi to carry the ark of the covenant of the LORD, to stand before the LORD to minister and to pronounce blessings in his name, as they still do today. [9]That is why the Levites have no share or inheritance among their

brothers; the LORD is their inheritance, as the LORD your God told them." (Deuteronomy 10:8, 9)

While the other tribes got to build homes, plant gardens, raise cattle and walk their land the Levites were called to a lifetime pilgrimage. They were sojourners in a strange new land. God said He was enough; He was their inheritance. They were called to be unattached to the things of the world.

> **"Since you call on a Father who judges each man's work impartially, live your lives as strangers here in reverent fear . . . ¹¹Dear friends, I urge you, as aliens and strangers in the world, to abstain from sinful desires, which war against your soul."**
> (1 PETER 1:17, 2:11)

This beautiful passage from Hebrews illustrates the unattached life God desires for His children/priests.

> **"By faith Abraham, when called to go to a place he would later receive as his inheritance, obeyed and went, even though he did not know where he was going. ⁹By faith he made his home in the Promised Land like a stranger in a foreign country; he lived in tents, as did Isaac and Jacob, who were heirs with him of the same promise. ¹⁰For he was looking forward to the city with foundations, whose architect and builder is God. ¹¹By faith Abraham, even though he was past age— and Sarah herself was barren—was enabled to become a father because he considered him faithful who had made the promise. ¹²And so from this one man, and he as good as dead, came descendants as numerous as the stars in the sky and**

as countless as the sand on the seashore. [13]All these people were still living by faith when they died. They did not receive the things promised; they only saw them and welcomed them from a distance. And they admitted that they were aliens and strangers on earth. [14]People who say such things show that they are looking for a country of their own. [15]If they had been thinking of the country they had left, they would have had opportunity to return. [16]Instead, they were longing for a better country—a heavenly one. Therefore God is not ashamed to be called their God, for he has prepared a city for them. " (Hebrews 11:8-16)

Just as the priests of old were anointed with oil and clothed by the high priest we too as believers have been set apart to be a different people, a people that live in the world but are not contaminated by it. We pass through but don't drive our tent pegs too deeply. We are simply not permanent fixtures here. Our citizenship is in another kingdom, one that will not pass away. That is a priestly lifestyle. Let's not get too attached here.

Now it's time to return to the tabernacle to finish the tour. Since only the priests could see what you will now see it was important that we talked about them. Up to now we have been in the sand with the smell of blood and the sound of dying but now we will pull back the curtain and enter a new world, a world of gold and sweet incense. Welcome to the Tent of Meeting and the first room, the Holy Place.

e you ever wondered?Have you eve
ndered?Have you ever wondered?H
. ever wondered?Have you ever won
ndered?Have you ever wondered?H
. ever wondered?Have you ever won
ndered?Have you ever wondered?H

- Why should we bother reading about all the rituals followd by the Old Testament priests? If we want to know about Jesus why not just read the New Testament?

CHAPTER 15

Holy Ground
REMOVE ALL SHOES

Once a sinner had completed his sacrifice at the Brazen Altar, he left the courtyard. Only the priests could go into the tabernacle tent. The priests had a duel role in substitution. They helped the sinner find peace with God by faith through the substitutionary death of the animal. Then they went before God with the blood of the sacrifice and offered it to Him on behalf of the sinner. They became the sinner's advocate, presenting his case before the judge. Only the priests were involved in the entire process.

The tent of meeting was located near the rear half of the courtyard and was a completely enclosed structure. Unlike the brass utensils found in the courtyard associated with death and judgment everything in the tent of meeting was made of gold.

The moment the priest stepped past the door or curtain of the tent he entered a quiet, beautiful golden room called the Holy Place. The sands were no longer covered in blood and sweet smelling incense filled the air. The contrast was striking.

Once inside the Holy Place the priest saw four things. On his left was a seven-armed lampstand. Its rich glow provided warm light to the golden walls. On the right side was a small golden table with 12 unleavened slabs of bread. Straight ahead on the far wall was a magnificent embroidered veil which hung from ceiling to floor. In front of the veil was a small golden altar with hot coals and incense burning on it. The room was stunning. Maybe it had something to do with the interior decorator, God Himself.

Beyond the veil at the end of the room was one more room, the Holy of Holies. Not even the priests went in there. The veil was the final barrier and only one man, the high priest, could go past it and only once per year. That is where the Ark of the Covenant was located and it is where God met with man through the person of the high priest. We will go behind the veil in the next chapter.

Not Your Usual Tent

Like other parts of the tabernacle the tent of meeting was a portable structure. It was made of wooden boards covered in gold and held together with

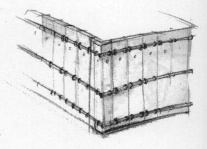

pins, poles and latches. The entire structure was 15 feet wide, 15 feet tall and 45 feet deep. It was divided into two rooms by the veil. The first room, the Holy Place, was 30 feet deep and the second room, on the other side of the veil, was a perfect cube, 15 feet by 15 feet by 15 feet.

After it was assembled by the priests it was covered by several layers of skins and cloths making the entire structure weather resistant and completely dark inside. The inside was shielded from the outside world.

As with other parts of the Levitical system we will be looking at the major items. There is much to learn in the small details and I hope you take time to do that later. Remember, God was the designer of this building and every-thing in it. There is a purpose behind every aspect of it.

The Golden Lampstand

This was the only source of light in the Holy Place. The second room had a different source of light, God's glory. The lampstand like the other pieces of furniture in the room was artistically fashioned from pure gold. God gave a clear description of its size and structure in His blueprints including the formula for the oil burned in its seven lamps.

> "Make a lampstand of pure, hammered gold. Make the entire lampstand and its decorations of one piece— the base, center stem, lamp cups, buds, and petals. [32]Make it with six branches going out from the center

stem, three on each side. ³³ Each of the six branches will have three lamp cups shaped like almond blossoms, complete with buds and petals. ³⁴ Craft the center stem of the lampstand with four lamp cups shaped like almond blossoms, complete with buds and petals. ³⁵ There will also be an almond bud beneath each pair of branches where the six branches extend from the center stem. ³⁶ The almond buds and branches must all be of one piece with the center stem, and they must be hammered from pure gold. ³⁷ Then make the seven lamps for the lampstand, and set them so they reflect their light forward. ³⁸ The lamp snuffers and trays must also be made of pure gold. ³⁹ You will need seventy-five pounds of pure gold for the lampstand and its accessories. ⁴⁰ "Be sure that you make everything according to the pattern I have shown you here on the mountain."

(Exodus 25:31-40)

It not only functioned in a practical way in providing light for the room but it also, like other parts of the tabernacle, pictured some aspect of Christ. When light is used as a symbol in Scripture it usually refers to truth and knowledge. Light dispels darkness and ignorance.

"When Jesus spoke again to the people, he said, "I am the light of the world. Whoever follows me will never walk in darkness, but will have the light of life." (John 8:12)

"This is the message we have heard from him and declare to you: God is light; in him there is no darkness at all." (1 John 1:5)

**"In him was life, and that life was the light of men.
⁹This was the true light that gives light to every man
who comes into the world."**
(John 1:4, 9)

**". . . the reason I was born and came into the world is
to testify to "the truth. Everyone on the side of truth
listens to me."** (John 18:37)

As a type it represented Christ as the ultimate, only source
of truth for man. The seven-fold nature of the lamp is usually
seen as a picture of the Holy Spirit. The book of Revelation uses
this image of the lampstand when describing Him:

**"From the throne came flashes of lightning and the
rumble of thunder. And in front of the throne were
seven torches with burning flames. This is the seven-
fold Spirit of God."**
(Revelation 4:5)

The lampstand was made of
pure gold. Only that metal
could serve as an adequate
picture of Deity. The tending
of the lampstand was a major
role of the high priest.

**"The LORD said to
Moses, ² "Command
the Israelites to bring
you clear oil of pressed olives for the light so that**

> the lamps may be kept burning continually. [3] Outside the curtain of the Testimony in the Tent of Meeting, Aaron is to tend the lamps before the LORD from evening till morning, continually. This is to be a lasting ordinance for the generations to come. [4] The lamps on the pure gold lampstand before the LORD must be tended continually." (Leviticus 4:1-4)

The book of Revelation gives us a beautiful description of Christ, our Great High Priest, walking about in the midst of seven golden lampstands.

> "When I turned to see who was speaking to me, I saw seven gold lampstands. [13] And standing in the middle of the lampstands was someone like the Son of Man. He was wearing a long robe with a gold sash across his chest." (Revelation 1:12.13)

The lampstands in this passage refer to the seven churches Christ addresses. Jesus is the light of the world and we who know Him are called to be light to the world as His ambassadors. We are commissioned to carry that light to all the nations. It is a priestly duty and a great privilege.

Remember: All this was about God's revealing His Messiah and His plan of redemption for His fallen creation. He has always wanted to bring His kids home. He alone is our source of truth, our sustainer, our access, our hope. He is our light.

A Table of Bread

Jesus is not only the light of the world, the way, the truth and

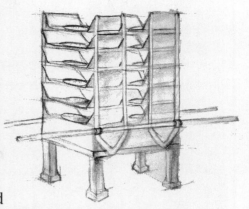

the life, but He is our suste-
nance, our Bread of Life. A
golden table of bread was on
the right side of the room. The
bread is referred to in Scripture as "showbread", or "face
bread." It literally means "bread
of the presence." The bread was always in the presence of God.
There were 12 loaves which represented the 12 tribes. So, even
though the tribes could not be physically present in the Holy
Place and stand before God they were there symbolically. The
loaves were eaten by the priests in the presence of God. It was
fellowship and communion by proxy for the people of Israel.
As with the other parts of the tabernacle the ingredients of the
bread was the best, fine flour. It was part of a greater picture
and it had to be pure.

> **"Our forefathers ate the manna in the desert; as it is
> written: 'He gave them bread from heaven to eat.'"
> [32]Jesus said to them, "I tell you the truth, it is not
> Moses who has given you the bread from heaven, but
> it is my Father who gives you the true bread from
> heaven. [33]For the bread of God is he who comes down
> from heaven and gives life to the world." [34]"Sir," they
> said, "from now on give us this bread." [35]Then Jesus
> declared, "I am the bread of life. He who comes to
> me will never go hungry, and he who believes in me
> will never be thirsty . . . [47]I tell you the truth, he who
> believes has everlasting life. [48]I am the bread of life.
> [49]Your forefathers ate the manna in the desert, yet
> they died. [50]But here is the bread that comes down
> from heaven, which a man may eat and not die."**
> (John 6:31-35, 47-50)

The priests ate the bread on a regular basis. This was a practical provision of food for the group who had no business to support them or fields to harvest. At the same time it pointed to the greater one, the provider of our daily bread.

The Veil

There was a great dividing curtain between the Holy Place and Holy of Holies. It was called the Veil of the Tabernacle.

> **"They made the curtain of blue, purple and scarlet yarn and finely twisted linen, with cherubim worked into it by a skilled craftsman."**
> (Exodus 36:35)

The cherubim were angelic guardians. They were first mentioned in Genesis and were found in the Garden of Eden. We will discuss them more in the next chapter. But just imagine these large majestic angelic guardians standing sentry on what is on the other side of the veil. The veil was the only thing

keeping man from direct access to God. Later when the temple was constructed it was made according to the same pattern as the tabernacle - only larger. All the same components were present in the temple including the veil. It was that veil in the temple that was torn in two when Jesus died.

> **"And Jesus cried out again with a loud voice, and
> yielded up His spirit. [51]And behold, the veil of the
> temple was torn in two from top to bottom; and the
> earth shook and the rocks were split."**
> (Matthew 27:50, 51)

Man was always separated from God because of sin. When sin
was eternally paid for by Christ on the cross the Scripture says
that "He who knew no sin was made to become sin for us." He
actually became our sin on the cross. In His flesh He bore our
sin and the eternal judgment of God in our place. When His
body was scourged, beaten and crucified He opened the way
for man to have fellowship with God. That which had separated
man from God was no longer in the way so God tore the veil
from top to bottom when Jesus said the words, "It is finished."

> **"Now where there is forgiveness of these things, there
> is no longer any offering for sin. [19]Therefore, breth-
> ren, since we have confidence to enter the holy place
> by the blood of Jesus, [20]by a new and living way which
> He inaugurated for us through the veil, that is, His
> flesh,"** (Hebrews 10:18-20)

The Altar of Incense

The final item in the holy place was the golden altar of incense
just in front of the veil. Its primary purpose was a place of
prayer. Even though man was physically separated from the actual presence of God he still had access to God through prayer.

Once a year the high priest could pass beyond the veil and
meet with God on the Day of Atonement. This was only after
his outer high priest garments were removed and he had made

sin offerings for himself and the people. Then, with a golden censor, he entered the Holy of Holies in a cloud of incense to approach the glory of God.

But daily at the golden altar the priests offered a small me-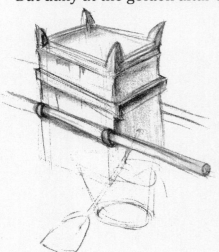morial portion of blood from the sacrifices along with sweet incense and prayer to God. This was as close as a man could get to God. The golden altar was the connection with God. Prayer today is still that most important connection with God. As believer priests we are called to a life of intercession for the lost, to bring their need before God.

The golden altar was the place where the intercessory prayer of the priest accompanied by blood and incense was accepted by God. The priest was like a defense attorney who presented the case to the judge, showing evidence that the crime was paid for so a pardon could be issued. Later, Jesus our Great High Priest is described as both defense attorney and judge and also the one who paid for the crime we committed.

> **"My dear children, I write this to you so that you will not sin. But if anybody does sin, we have one who speaks to the Father in our defense—Jesus Christ, the Righteous One. [2]He is the atoning sacrifice for our sins, and not only for ours but also for the sins of the whole world."** (1 John 2:1-2)

> **"O LORD, I call to you; come quickly to me. Hear my**

voice when I call to you. May my prayer be set before you like incense; may the lifting up of my hands be like the evening sacrifice." (Psalm 141:1.2)

When John described the heavenly scene in the book of Revelation he revealed a scene very much like what we see in the holy place.

"Another angel, who had a golden censer, came and stood at the altar. He was given much incense to offer, with the prayers of all the saints, on the golden altar before the throne."
(Revelation 8:3)

The hot coals and frequent prayer of the priests serves as an example to us of what God loves. He loves His kids to say, "I am glad You are my Dad." We are exhorted in the Scripture to be fervent and effectual in our prayer life. After all, we have the light of the world, the bread of life, heavenly guardians, a high priest who "ever lives to make intercession for us" and my heavenly Father who loves nothing better than to spend time with His children.

With that thought it is time to go behind the veil into the Holy of Holies.

ve you ever wondered?Have you eve
ndered?Have you ever wondered?H
ever wondered?Have you ever won
ndered?Have you ever wondered?H
ever wondered?Have you ever won
ndered?**Have you ever wondered?**H

- What was the purpose of those Cherubim in the Garden of Eden and what were they?

- What happened to the Tree of Life?

CHAPTER 16

The Summit Meeting
THE HOLY OF HOLIES - THE ROOM AT THE BACK

If there was ever a time to take our shoes off I guess this would be the time. We enter holy ground. Only the high priest saw what we will be looking at and only once a year. The Ark of the Covenant may not have been seen when it was moved. When the veil was taken down it is probable it was draped over the Ark of the Covenant. The Ark was then carried through the desert with poles on the shoulders of the priests. It is uncertain if the ark was covered while being transported. One tradition has it covered the entire time with a blue cloth and others see it transported but uncovered and visible by the people. The word translated atonement cover is also translated "veil" by another version.

Remember, God never told man to build a place where He could live with man. The tabernacle was designed to show man the way that he could be made right with God and then

God could meet with man. The tabernacle was not really about where God and man could fellowship but how. It was through the cross that God and man are reconciled and the tabernacle was the cross in the Old Testament. God told man to make a picture of the way He would meet with man. And that meeting place was ultimately at the mercy seat of the Ark of the Covenant. That is where the blood was accepted by God and justice satisfied. Let's look at that Ark.

Israel's Hope Chest

The Ark of the Covenant was an unusual object and one of great beauty. It was Israel's hope chest. Constructed like a chest it was about two feet wide by two feet high and around four feet long. I say "around" because the dimensions were given in cubits and a cubit was the distance from the tip of the longest finger to the person's elbow. That distance varied by individual. The Ark rested on four feet and had rings and permanent poles for transporting it just like the other items in the Holy Place. It was made of acacia wood and covered with pure gold. Like a chest, it was open on the top and a lid, called the Atonement Cover or Mercy Seat, with two sculpted, golden cherubim covered the opening.

Three items were kept inside.

> **"This ark contained the gold jar of manna, Aaron's staff that had budded, and the stone tablets of the covenant."** (Hebrews 9:4)

The gold pot that contained a memorial portion of manna was there to remind the people that man "shall not live by bread alone but by every word that proceeds from the mouth of God shall man live." Aaron's rod that budded was a reminder that God had chosen Aaron as His priest and God does not tolerate rebellion. The story of Korah's rebellion which resulted in the budding of Aaron's rod can be read in Numbers 16.

> **"And the Lord said to Moses: "Place Aaron's staff permanently before the Ark of the Covenant to serve as a warning to rebels. This should put an end to their complaints against me and prevent any further deaths."** (Numbers 17:10)

The final item inside the Ark of the Covenant was the stone tablets, the Ten Commandments. But there is more to this than just stone. The tablets were in essence the broken law of God. Man had no sooner been given the moral law when he broke that law. God had the broken law placed in a very particular place. It had to do with what was above the chest, the Mercy Seat where blood was sprinkled and God was satisfied. The broken law was covered by the blood of the sacrifice and God forgave the people. Once again we see the story of grace that is so abundantly clear in the Old Testament.

After the Ark was filled with the three items the atonement cover was placed over the top opening. Like the other parts, it was gold (actually all the gold items were artistically fashioned in acacia wood and overlaid in gold). The final appearance was solid gold.

On the Mercy Seat there were two angels, cherubim, fashioned into the cover so it was one piece. The cherubim were on the outside of the cover with wings extended up and covering the Mercy Seat. They were heavenly sentinels, guardians of the place where atonement was made for the sins of the people.

"The cherubim are to have their wings spread upward, overshadowing the cover with them. The cherubim are to face each other, looking toward the cover. [21] Place the cover on top of the ark and put in the ark the Testimony, which I will give you. [22] There, above the cover between the two cherubim that are over the ark of the Testimony, I will meet with you and give you all my commands for the Israelites."
(Exodus 25:20-22)

"The LORD reigns, let the nations tremble; he sits enthroned between the cherubim, let the earth shake. [8] O LORD our God, you answered them; you were to Israel a forgiving God..." (Psalm 99:1,8)

The Mercy Seat was just that, the place of mercy. The theological word that describes the mercy seat was the place of propitiation or place of satisfaction. God was satisfied with the blood of the sacrifice offered in faith. This is because it all pointed to the final sacrifice that pleased God.

> **"But it was the Lord's good plan to crush him and cause him grief Yet when his life is made an offering for sin, he will have many descendants. He will enjoy a long life, and the Lord's good plan will prosper in his hands. [11] When he sees all that is accomplished by his anguish, he will be satisfied. And because of his experience, my righteous servant will make it possible for many to be counted righteous, for he will bear all their sins."** (Isaiah 53:10,11)

It was there at the Ark and specifically the Mercy Seat that the high priest offered a sin offering for the nation of Israel on the annual Day of Atonement. On that day he took off his high priestly garments, only wearing the white undergarment when he went beyond the veil. He first offered a Sin Offering for himself and then he did it for all the people. God met him at the Mercy Seat and the blood covered the broken law for all the people. It was also at the Mercy Seat that God would manifest His presence and give His statutes and instructions to His people. It was literally the Throne of God in the Theocracy of Israel. On the next page these two concepts will be merged.

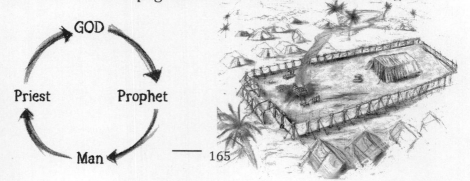

GOD

Priest   Prophet

Man

165

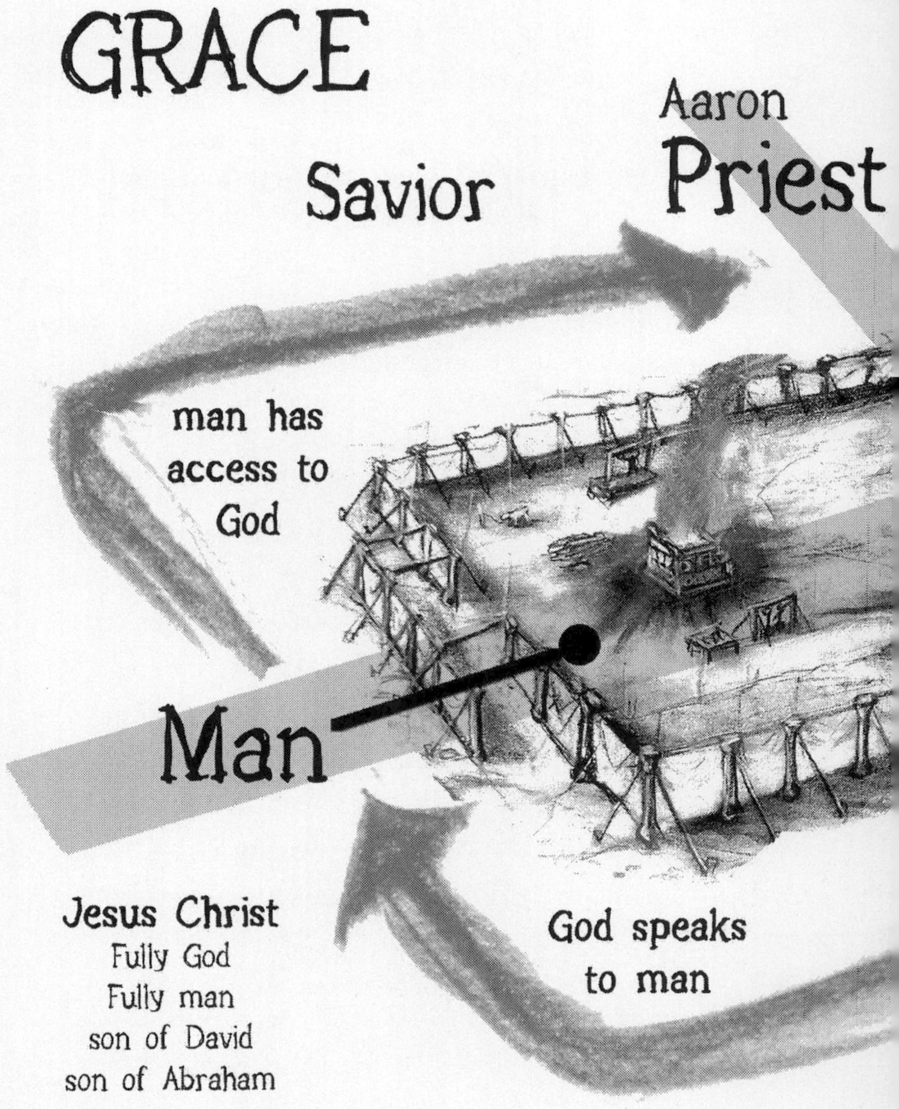

GRACE

Savior

Aaron
Priest

man has
access to
God

Man

Jesus Christ
Fully God
Fully man
son of David
son of Abraham

God speaks
to man

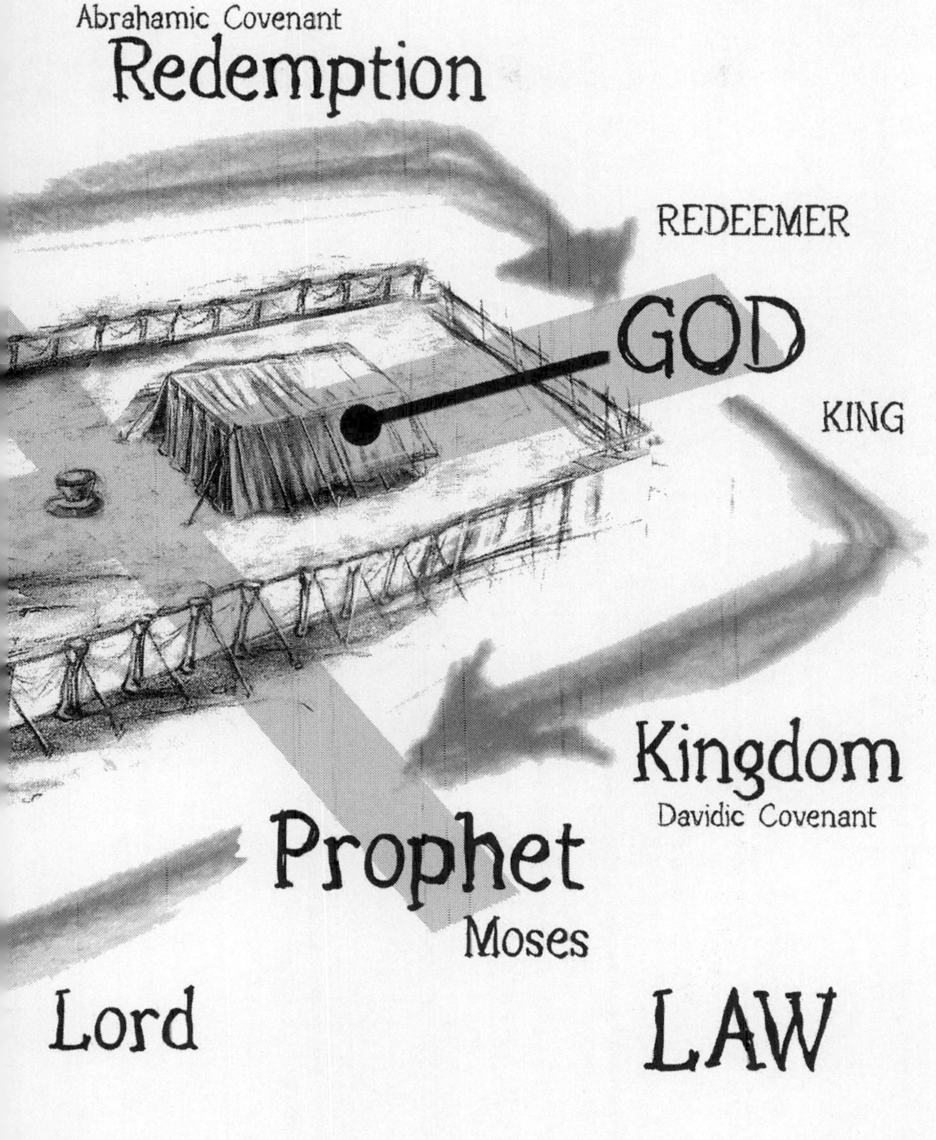

Abrahamic Covenant
Redemption

REDEEMER

GOD

KING

Kingdom
Davidic Covenant

Prophet
Moses

Lord

LAW

The tabernacle presented a complete picture. It showed law and grace, kingdom and redemption, priest and prophet, Lord and Savior, Abraham and David and religious and civil. It was a complete picture of God's two-fold plan of Redemption and Kingdom. It was God's greatest object lesson of His one unchanging plan of redemption from the beginning of time.

Guardian Angels

Don't misunderstand this title. I am not talking about angels God has sent to protect you. There was another "Guardian" type of angel, the Cherubim. The word Cherub or Cherubim is used 69 times in the Bible. The first usage in found in Genesis 3. The other 68 uses all refer to the same thing, namely, the word describes very special angels stationed at the Mercy Seat of the Ark of the Covenant. That was the place where the blood of the offering was applied and God was satisfied. It is reasonable to expect that the usage of the word in Genesis 3 would be the same as the other 68 uses. If that is true then the Cherubim mentioned in Genesis 3 will have something to do with being guardians of the spot where sacrifice and blood and God meet and God is satisfied. In the early days before the complete Levitical system was in view, the places where all these things happened was at the stone altars where the patriarchs offered their burnt offerings for sin.

With this in mind let's revisit the first time we see those celestial guardians. It is in the Garden of Eden. Man had fallen and God had cursed the man, the woman, the serpent and the earth. Read it very carefully.

> **"The LORD God made garments of skin for Adam and his wife and clothed them. [22] And the LORD God said, "The man has now become like one of us, knowing good and evil. He must not be allowed to reach out his hand and take also from the tree of life and eat, and live forever." [23] So the LORD God banished him from the Garden of Eden to work the ground from which he had been taken. [24] After he drove the man out, he placed on the east side of the Garden of Eden cherubim and a flaming sword flashing back and forth to guard the way to the tree of life."** (Genesis 3:21-24)

Maybe it is the Sunday school drawings or artists paintings that have given us our perspective on this scene. We often see Adam and Eve sad and dejected leaving the garden as an angel with a great sword sends them away. The inference is that they can never come back. The reason is usually given that once man had tasted sin God could not allow him to live forever in that fallen state. So he was banned from returning to the tree of life where he would eat from it and live forever in his sinful state.

Now, certainly parts of that are true but the basic plan of God is often missed. Remember what we have been talking about throughout the book? God is a God of love and His greatest desire is for man to be brought back into a right relationship with Him and to know eternal life. God wants man to ultimately eat of the tree of life and that is what we see on the new earth in the book of Revelation.

> **"Then the angel showed me the river of the water of life, as clear as crystal, flowing from the throne of God and of the Lamb [2]down the middle of the great street of the city. On each side of the river stood the tree of life, bearing twelve crops of fruit, yielding its fruit**

every month. And the leaves of the tree are for the healing of the nations. ³No longer will there be any curse. The throne of God and of the Lamb will be in the city, and his servants will serve him."
(Revelation 22:1-3)

I have a good friend who knows what the Tree of Life looks like. How do I know this? Because my friend died and is with Jesus and that is where the Tree of Life is today. All believers will one day eat of the tree of life and live forever on the new earth in fellowship with God and each other. That has been what God has desired from the beginning. So when man fell it was God's plan to provide a way for man to get to the tree of life. What was that way? You should be able to answer that by now. It was through the cross of Christ. The cross was the way to God, the way to the Tree of Life. Our enemy, Satan, does not want us to have access to that tree. He wants us lost for eternity.

When man fell in the Garden of Eden God killed the first animal. Adam and Eve began from then on to understand the necessity of sacrifice and atonement. They saw God kill that animal, probably a lamb, to cover their sinful hearts and cursed bodies with the bloody skin. An altar was set up where Adam and Even taught their sons to offer sacrifices for sin. As long as man approached God through the blood and by faith he could find life, he could find his way to the Tree of Life in heaven one day. No, he could not eat of the tree yet while still in his fallen state but the way to the tree was protected by God.

Now, that is why we see the cherubim. We have seen that they are guardians of the Mercy Seat, the place where blood was sprinkled, God was satisfied and man forgiven. They were no doubt stationed first in the garden for the same purpose. They guarded the place where the altar was, the place where blood was shed, God satisfied and man forgiven. God did not angrily send sinful man away from His presence and the Tree of Life. Just the opposite. When man sinned God went looking for him. God sacrificed that first animal.

Although not directly stated this is the time that the first altar in history would have been set up. Later Adam and Eve would go to that place to offer burnt offerings as sin offerings and teach their two sons to do the same. That first altar was probably placed near the entrance of the garden they were banished from. Although they could not yet physically go back to the Tree of Life they understood that through the blood they could find forgiveness and one day they would eat again from the Tree of Life. God stationed His heavenly sentries at the altar to resist the enemy and keep the way open for man to have eternal life, to guard the way to the Tree of Life.

Man would always have a way back to the tTree of Life if he came God's way, through the blood. Now, read the Genesis passage again.

> **"So the LORD God banished him from the Garden of Eden to work the ground from which he had been taken. 24 After he drove the man out, he placed on the east side of the Garden of Eden cherubim and a flaming sword flashing back and forth <u>to guard the way to the tree of life.</u>"**
> (Genesis 3:23, 24, emphasis mine)

Read the words of Bible expositor, Donald Barnhouse:

> *"The first contradiction I ever found was that which exists between God's express command to Moses, "Thou shalt not make unto thee any graven image" (Exodus 20:4), and the Lord's almost immediate command for Moses to make graven images of two cherubim of gold, "of beaten work shalt thou make them, in the two ends of the mercy seat. And make one cherub on the one end, and the other cherub on the other end; even of the mercy seat shall ye make the cherubim on the two ends thereof"(Exodus 25:18, 19). It was not until I came to realize that God had designed to have on the mercy seat the representation of the altar at the door of the Garden of Eden, with the cherubim, which protected the way to the tree of life, that I knew the inner meaning of that representation. Satan would never be able to block the access of the one who came through the way of the cross."*

The love of God is clearly seen from the very beginning. He responds in grace to his erring children. He provides everything necessary for them to find their way home. Stay close to Jesus and He will lead you home. He was the lamb slain from before the foundation of the world.

Remember our study on progressive revelation? In the Garden of Eden we have a primitive tabernacle. We have substitution, a sacrificial animal, an altar and even a primitive Ark of the Covenant with the Cherubim. When blood was shed on the altar it was the Mercy Seat of God, the place where God was satisfied. God always provided a way for His prodigals to return. So even though progressive revelation revealed more and more to man as the years went by, the first man had a clear understanding of many things. He knew how to find his way home by faith.

Remember, this is all one story. It is the story of God's unchanging plan of redemption for His rebellious people. It is an old story. It is a current story. It is still the same story. Man is still sinful, God is still loving and there is still a way home no matter if we are stranded in a garden, a desert or a modern city.

———————

And God is still holy and he honors His unchanging word. Here is a true, modern day account from OMF missionaries Allan and Evelyn Crane that show that God's word is forever. They worked in Thailand and wrote this general letter to their supporters in 1974.

"God has been speaking to the young people in a very strong and fearsome manner... Some weeks back I had a letter from a pastor in North Burma that gave me news I could hardly believe. But then came another letter from a pastor and then another, all giving the same shocking news so that I had to believe what seemed unbelievable. And while in Thailand I talked this over with Isaiah (a co-worker) and he confirmed all the details, and even giving more, for this event happened on Easter Sunday morning when the Lisu gather for their Joyful Festival.

Some of the young people got together and decided to go off into the jungle. They had collected some rice whiskey and some "smokes" as they call them in Lisu, and so off they went young men and women in their late teens and early 20s. When they had drunk all their whiskey and finished all their "smokes" they played an old heathen game of the boys calling riddles to the girls, and the girls having to guess the meaning. It is full of impure suggestions. Then they foolishly called on God saying, "Oh God, you can do all things, send us some more whiskey and some more smokes" Just a few minutes later tigers came out of the surrounding Jungle and attacked them, killing 24 of them. The rest escaped back to the village with the news.

Immediately the whole village was in an uproar and the Easter meetings all suspended. Some of them went off to a nearby army camp and reported the incident and they then went into the jungle. They found 20 bodies but four they did not find. They also shot one or two tigers. This has sent ripples of fear and a sense of the nearness of the God of Heaven whose name is not to be played with.

Indeed the whole matter is going over the district, for tigers do not normally act like this, they do not travel in numbers nor usually do they attack at all unless it is an old tiger who cannot find the fast-running game he's used to and now attacks humans. But this was all out of the usual picture and more than ever evident that God was speaking to the young people who have foolishly turned to the attractions of the world around and also to their parents who realize that they have been slack and not taught them as they should nor been as keen in the things of the Lord as they ought. Pray that this will indeed bring about a sincere repentance among many young Lisu all through the Lisu country whether in Burma or Thailand, wherever this news spreads . . .

Leviticus 26; 21, 22 says "And if you walk contrary to Me and will not hearken to Me... I will send wild beasts among you which shall rob you of your children." (OMF missionaries Allan and Evelyn Crane, 1974)

It is a sobering story but illustrates that God has not changed. He is holy and must judge sin. But He is also loving and gracious to all who repent and seek Him. This hope has not changed since the beginning of time.

Now, It's time to head to a feast. The last section of this book will complete our journey. It will be our final glimpse into the shadows. You may need your sunglasses again for this one, the light is pretty bright.

SECTION 5

The Feast Seasons

God loves a good celebration. Remember how the father of the prodigal celebrated when his wayward son came home? And we know the angels rejoice when one sinner repents. One day God is going to host the dinner party of all time, the marriage supper of the lamb.

God set up the feasts of Israel. The seven feasts inaugurated in Leviticus 23 served several purposes. Some represented serious times of introspection and personal cleansing while others were a time of rejoicing as a nation when the crops came in. The individual feasts were organized into three main feast seasons and the entire nation gathered to celebrate and worship. The feasts became the thread that held the fabric of Israel together over the centuries to follow.

These gatherings were nation-builders drawing the people closer together. First they helped the nation economically.

Trade took place. Those who lived far off journeyed to Jerusalem for the three feast seasons. They exchanged products, ideas and stories. The feasts also had national value. The Jewish nation bonded as they spent time together experiencing the unity and diversity they had as a people. The feasts were also a source of great religious value as well. The people recounted together the stories of their faith. Since the feasts themselves were historically centered they were a reminder of what God had done and the miracle they were as a nation.

They were faith-building times for families keeping their heritage alive. The 12 tribes eventually lived in different regions but three times a year they all came together to celebrate who they were and their God.

> **"Three times a year all your men must appear before the LORD your God at the place he will choose: at the Feast of Unleavened Bread, the Feast of Weeks and the Feast of Tabernacles. No man should appear before the LORD empty handed: [17] Each of you must bring a gift in proportion to the way the LORD your God has blessed you."**
> (Deuteronomy 16:16, 17)

Fifteen of the Psalms were written for the people to sing as they traveled to Jerusalem. These songs of the journey are often called Songs of Ascents or Degrees. Songs like Psalm 121 and 122 could be heard as the pilgrims climbed the hills outside of Jerusalem looking towards its golden sunlit skyline:

"I lift up my eyes to the hills—where does my help come from? [2] My help comes from the LORD, the Maker of heaven and earth. [3] He will not let your foot slip— he who watches over you will not slumber;"
(Psalm 121:1-3)

"I rejoiced with those who said to me, "Let us go to the house of the LORD." [2] Our feet are standing in your gates, O Jerusalem. [3] Jerusalem is built like a city that is closely compacted together."
(Psalm 122:1-3)

But the most important part of the feasts was in the shadows. Like all other parts of the Levitical System, the feasts were about Christ. They painted a picture of the person who was yet to come as Israel's Redeemer, Savior and the King of the whole world.

Each of the next three chapters will look at one feast season. The first season, Unleavened Bread, had three distinct feasts that were celebrated. The second season had one feast and the third season had three. They had a very significant chronological sequence concerning Christ. But then that should not surprise us. We will examine them in the exact order God gave them which is also the order in which they appear on the Jewish calendar.

Our first stop is a night that was different from all other nights.

ve you ever wondered?Have you eve
ndered?Have you ever wondered?H
ever wondered?Have you ever wor
ndered?Have you ever wondered?H
ever wondered?Have you ever wor
ndered?**Have you ever wondered?**H

- We know the death of Christ is pictured in the Old Testament but where do we find the resurrection of Christ?

CHAPTER 17

Night screams and a midnight noon

THE SEASON OF PASSOVER AND THE CROSS

It's review time again. No, I am not going to say what has been said over and over again in this book. God is going to do it. I guess He knew we have short memories as fallen people so He kept giving us different pictures to say the same thing. One might come to the conclusion that He was tying to get a point across that He was doing something special and wanted it to be clear. But people still had trouble getting it.

Read this fascinating story that happened right after the resurrection of Jesus and pay attention to His response to the two travelers:

> "Now that same day two of them were going to a village called Emmaus, about seven miles from Jerusalem. [14]They were talking with each other about everything that had happened. [15]As they talked and

discussed these things with each other, Jesus himself came up and walked along with them; [16]but they were kept from recognizing him. [17]He asked them, "What are you discussing together as you walk along?" They stood still, their faces downcast. [18]One of them, named Cleopas, asked him, "Are you only a visitor to Jerusalem and do not know the things that have happened there in these days?" [19]"What things?" he asked. "About Jesus of Nazareth," they replied. "He was a prophet, powerful in word and deed before God and all the people. [20]The chief priests and our rulers handed him over to be sentenced to death, and they crucified him; [21]but we had hoped that he was the one who was going to redeem Israel. And what is more, it is the third day since all this took place. [22]In addition, some of our women amazed us. They went to the tomb early this morning [23]but didn't find his body. They came and told us that they had seen a vision of angels, who said he was alive. [24]Then some of our companions went to the tomb and found it just as the women had said, but him they did not see." [25]He said to them, "How foolish you are, and how slow of heart to believe all that the prophets have spoken! [26]Did not the Christ have to suffer these things and then enter his glory?" [27]And beginning with Moses and all the Prophets, he explained to them what was said in all the Scriptures concerning himself." (Luke 24:13-27)

Let me see if I can paraphrase this. Jesus was saying, "I am the Messiah, the Promised One from the beginning. Remember all the pictures and hints you were given for several thousands of years? Remember the Passover, the serpent on the pole, the brazen altar and a gazillion other pictures God gave you? How could you not see that I was to come, be born of a virgin, die on a Roman cross and be resurrected? Did you celebrate the feasts and not see it?

You just had the Passover a few days ago, what did it mean to you that a lamb was killed and the blood was put on the door-posts of the house in Moses' day? You just celebrated the feast of first fruits on Sunday. What were you thinking it was all about? Since you were young you have gone to the temple and participated in sin and guilt offerings. Why are you shocked that the One who is your Savior should die as a sacrificial lamb for your sins? It was pictured all along. This was all part of God's one unchanging plan of redemption. I think that is what was contained in His words, "How foolish you are . . ."

Remember those two words, Redemption and Kingdom? They are God's two-fold program. He is coming for His people and He is coming for his stuff. Well, guess what the feasts are all about? Yes, you guessed it, Redemption and Kingdom. Jesus is King and Redeemer, both Lord and Christ.

One Important Point Before we Start

Before we look at the seven feasts it is important to understand one thing. Jesus came to earth and one day He is coming again. He first came to specifically deal with the issue of sin. He came as our Savior and one day He will come again to finish the complete picture. He will reign as King of Kings and Lord of Lords on a new earth. Even though each of these comings has a specific focus or purpose that does not mean He is not fully Redeemer and fully King at all times. He has never ceased being both King and Redeemer. When He was born in a manger the purpose of His coming was to die and He died as the Lamb of God. But He was still King of Kings and Lord of Lords. When

He came He was King and Redeemer and He is coming again as King and Redeemer.

> **"Therefore let all Israel be assured of this: God has made this Jesus, whom you crucified, both Lord and Christ."** (Acts 2:36)

Now let's look at the seven feasts. The general term for the first feast season is the Feast of Unleavened Bread. It consisted of three individual feasts, Passover, Unleavened Bread and the feast of First Fruits. They were all three celebrated during a one week observance. We begin with the first one, Passover.

The night that was different from all other nights (Feast 1 - Passover)

There are very few types or pictures of the sacrificial death of the Lamb of God in the Scriptures that are clearer than the Passover. Remember that first Passover when the children of Israel huddled in fear inside their homes in Egypt? The screams of the Egyptians echoed across the city as the angel of the Lord slaughtered the first born of each household in the land. Only the homes with the blood of a lamb covering their doorways were spared. It was a night of terror

"and when I see the blood, I will pass over you."
(Exodus 12:13)

but also a night of redemption.

The word "redemption" means to buy back. It is the same as when a person gives up something he owns to a pawn shop in exchange for a few coins. That act of desperation is often foolish but it is a choice and a legal transaction. If that person wishes to get the pawned item back he has to return the money along with a fee to redeem it. Man was created to be God's special possession but he sold himself to the slave market of sin. Unfortunately, for man, the redemption cost to buy his freedom back was too steep. So God Himself paid the ransom, the complete cost, to free man from slavery.

The Hebrew children were slaves in Egypt with no hope of breaking the bondage. God Himself delivered them with a mighty hand. The plagues He sent on Egypt made Pharaoh tear up the contract and let the people go. The final decisive act that freed the people and brought them out of bondage was the Passover. The price of redemption was the blood of a spotless lamb that was slain. Just like in the Garden of Eden when God used the blood to cover sin, here He used the blood of the Lamb to protect and deliver His children.

God set up a permanent celebration of the Passover to remind his people that he is a God of deliverance and that the blood of the lamb covers and protects from judgment. The New Testament leaves no doubt that the Passover lamb points to Jesus:

> **"When Jesus had finished saying all these things, he said to his disciples, [2]"As you know, the Passover is two days away— and the Son of Man will be handed over to be crucified."** (Matthew 26:1, 2)

> "Get rid of the old yeast that you may be a new batch without yeast—as you really are. For Christ, our Passover lamb, has been sacrificed."
>
> (1 Corinthians 5:7)

The Passover night of horror happened again on Calvary. This time the Angel of Judgment stopped at the cross and only one first born died, the Son of God. Noon became like midnight and Christ's cry of anguish rattled the far ends of the universe.

> "At noon, darkness fell across the whole land until three o'clock. [34] Then at three o'clock Jesus called out with a loud voice, "Eloi, Eloi, lema sabachthani?" which means "My God, my God, why have you abandoned me?" (Mark 15:33, 34)

The final Lamb of God had come to take away the sin of the world. Thousands of lambs and altars pointed to this moment. The temple flowed with blood during the Passover season. Jesus Himself would have seen the fresh blood as He was led to Calvary.

God the Son, had become man, sinless and holy and now He actually became the sin of the world. The Father could no longer look at His own Son. Jesus cried out that He was abandoned, alone. The sin of man separated the Father and the Son for the first time in eternal history. God bore the penalty of our sin.

> "God made him who had no sin to be sin for us, so that in him we might become the righteousness of God." (2 Corinthians 5:21)

Jesus didn't just die for us, He died as us. An old southern spiritual asks, "Were you there when they crucified my Lord?" The answer is yes.

The death of Christ happened during the Passover feast season. The last supper of Christ the night before His crucifixion was the annual Passover meal. The death of our Savior took place on the same edge of the mountain where God stopped Abraham from sacrificing his son by providing a substitute. It all happened outside the gate of the temple where sin offerings were in progress. God had said that the sin offering was to be carried outside the gate because it was a despicable thing. Jesus had become that despicable thing. He did it for us. Have you thanked Him recently?

The Jewish people today still celebrate the feast of Passover. They begin their meal with the youngest child asking the question, "Why is this night different from all other nights?" Then they recount the great deliverance God accomplished through the blood of the lamb. And they look for their Messiah. But He came and went to the cross. If you have never trusted Him as your Passover Lamb now would be a very good time to do that. If you do so, I can promise you that this night will be different from all others.

A Real House Cleaning – (Feast 2 - Unleavened Bread)
During the entire week the feast of Unleavened Bread was carried out even while celebrating Passover and First Fruits. In some ways Unleavened Bread was a condition of the heart and home. During the week all leaven or yeast was removed from

the home. There were even games the children played to try to find it. It was a time of purification.

When leaven (yeast) is used in the Bible as a symbol, it represents something that permeates or penetrates. It can represent something good like the Kingdom of God and how it spreads in the darkness of this world. Leaven is also used as a symbol for evil or sin like when Jesus warned about the leaven of the Pharisees. It is used in this fashion in the Feast of Unleavened Bread. Yeast permeates dough and makes it rise. It only takes a little to infiltrate the entire loaf. So it is used to symbolize the wide spread effect or damage even a small amount of sin can cause.

> "Your boasting is not good. Do you not know that a little leaven leavens the whole lump of dough? [7]Clean out the old leaven so that you may be a new lump, just as you are in fact unleavened. For Christ our Passover also has been sacrificed. [8]Therefore let us celebrate the feast, not with old leaven, nor with the leaven of malice and wickedness, but with the unleavened bread of sincerity and truth."
>
> (1 Corinthians 5:6-8)

Throughout the feasts of Passover and First Fruits the people's heart was to be set apart and single-minded on the Lord. Sin was to be consciously put aside. As a type of Christ it was a picture of His sinless life, without leaven. As the spotless Lamb of God He was qualified to be the Passover Lamb for the whole world.

Bringing in the Sheaves (Feast 3 - First Fruits)

Leviticus 23:8-14 gives the instructions for the Feast of First Fruits.

"¹⁰When you enter the land I am going to give you and you reap its harvest, bring to the priest a sheaf of the first grain you harvest. ¹¹ He is to wave the sheaf before the LORD so it will be accepted on your behalf; the priest is to wave it <u>on the day after the Sabbath,"</u>

(Leviticus 23:10,11)

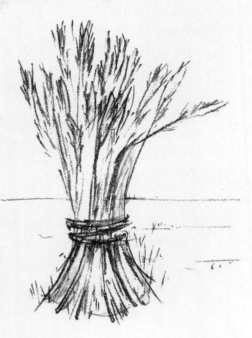

Not just the day after the Sabbath but specifically the day after the Passover Sabbath. That is the Sunday after the celebration of Passover. Jesus died on the cross during the annual Passover celebration. What happened on Sunday after that Passover? Yes, that was the resurrection. The feast of First Fruits was a celebration of the beginning of the harvest; the very first of the new crop was offered and a pledge was made of more to come of the same variety. Jesus was the first fruits of the new crop and his pledge was that the greater harvest was coming.

"But Christ has indeed been raised from the dead, the firstfruits of those who have fallen asleep. ²¹For since death came through a man, the resurrection of the dead comes also through a man. ²²For as in Adam all die, so in Christ all will be made alive. ²³But each in his own turn: Christ, the firstfruits; then, when he comes, those who belong to him."

(1 Corinthians 15:20-23)

"He chose to give us birth through the word of truth, that we might be a kind of firstfruits of all he created."
(James 1:18)

Remember what Jesus told those two travelers on the road to Emmaus? He said that if they had believed what Moses had written they would have understood that He would die and be resurrected. The actual day of His resurrection was recorded in the Feast of First Fruits, the Sunday after the Passover Sabbath.

So, what is this new crop, this new variety Jesus represented? Well, Jesus was not the first one to be raised from the dead. Lazarus and others came back from the dead. But Jesus was the first to be resurrected to never die again. He rose in His resurrection body and so shall we who know Him as Savior. Jesus is the beginning of the new crop. And His resurrection is a pledge of the coming harvest, a new crop after His kind.

"Dear friends, now we are children of God, and what we will be has not yet been made known. But we know that when he appears, we shall be like him, for we shall see him as he is."
(1 John 3:2)

We will be like him, resurrected in new bodies never to know death again. The first three feasts were a chronological prophecy of our sinless savior, his death and resurrection. 50 days after the Resurrection of Christ the next event on the prophetic calendar was scheduled, the Feast of Weeks or Pentecost.

re you ever wondered?Have you eve
ndered?Have you ever wondered?H
ever wondered?Have you ever won
ndered?Have you ever wondered?H
ever wondered?Have you ever won
ndered?Have you ever wondered?H

- Why did Jesus wait over a month after His resurrection before the church was born at Pentecost?

- What is the meaning of Pentecost?

CHAPTER 18

The Wind of Harvest
PENTECOST - THE FEAST OF WEEKS

Most Christians are familiar with the New Testament account of the Day of Pentecost. We associate it with a new beginning, the official start of the church. But Pentecost did not start in the New Testament. It was actually the fourth feast or second feast season in the Jewish calendar. The word "Pente" means 50. It gets its name because it comes 50 days after the feast of First Fruits.

First Fruits was when the people of Israel offered the first of their new crop to the Lord in thanksgiving, making a pledge of more to come at harvest time. 50 days later the full harvest came in and the celebration of that event was the Feast of Weeks or Pentecost. It was the time of ingathering. This feast took place in April or May depending on the calendar.

Now we pick up the story in the New Testament book of Acts. Christ has died and resurrected. This all happened during the

Feast of Unleavened Bread. He has appeared to many since the resurrection.

> **"After his suffering, he showed himself to these men and gave many convincing proofs that he was alive. He appeared to them over a period of forty days and spoke about the kingdom of God. [4]On one occasion, while he was eating with them, he gave them this command: "Do not leave Jerusalem, but wait for the gift my Father promised, which you have heard me speak about."** (Acts 1:3.4)

The Disciples were all Jewish so they celebrated the traditional feasts. They knew that the Feast of Pentecost was close at hand. Jesus had just explained to them the true meaning of the Feasts so they gathered with great anticipation for the next event on the prophetic calendar of God, Pentecost, the Feast of Ingathering.

> **"And when the day of Pentecost had fully come, they were all assembled together in one place."**
> (Amplified Bible, Acts 2:1)

Even though the feast of Pentecost had been celebrated for over a thousand years, it had an ultimate purpose like the other feasts of pointing to Christ. It accomplished its purpose the day the New Testament Church was born. The day of Pentecost had finally fully come.

It was the great day of ingathering. Following the outpouring of the Holy Spirit on the believers, God began to do mighty works among the people and many came to faith. 3,000 believed the first day. The body of Christ was growing; the harvest had begun and that harvest continues to this day.

These first four feasts were in absolute chronology. Passover pictured the sacrificial death of the Lamb of God. First Fruits pictured His resurrection and unleavened bread revealed His sinless nature. Pentecost revealed the glorification of Christ and the birth of the body of Christ, the New Testament Church.

It would be expected that the final feast season, which contained three feasts, would also be chronological and that is exactly right. When Jesus came and died on the cross He came as the son of Abraham to be God's sacrificial lamb. He came as the Redeemer of the world. Our King is our Redeemer. He is coming again to lay final claim to His rightful throne as the Son of David, the King of Kings and Lord of Lords. Our Redeemer is our King.

That is what the final feasts are primarily about, His Kingdom program and His second coming. But before that final feast season happens there is a long gap in the Jewish calendar. The first four feasts were all connected in one rapid fire sequence, taking place in less than 60 days. Then there is a long wait before the last feast week.

Today we are standing in the gap. But one day, and possibly soon, the silence will be broken. How did the Jews announce the beginning of the last feast season? With a loud and long trumpet blast. Let's see how it all ends.

CHAPTER 19

What a Blast!

THE FEAST SEASON OF TABERNACLES

Jesus has never stopped being King of Kings and Lord of Lords but He will yet one day have His coronation day. That will happen when He comes again. He came the first time to redeem His children and He is coming again to officially reclaim His kingdom. He is both Redeemer and Reclaimer. Here is how His second coming will be announced:

> "At that time the sign of the Son of Man will appear in the sky, and all the nations of the earth will mourn. They will see the Son of Man coming on the clouds of the sky, with power and great glory. 31And he will send his angels with a loud trumpet call, and they will gather his elect from the four winds, from one end of the heavens to the other." (Matthew 24:30-31)

"For the Lord himself will come down from heaven, with a loud command, with the voice of the archangel and with the trumpet call of God, and the dead in Christ will rise first. [17]After that, we who are still alive and are left will be caught up together with them in the clouds to meet the Lord in the air. And so we will be with the Lord forever. [18]Therefore encourage each other with these words."

(1 Thessalonians 3:16-18)

"Listen, I tell you a mystery: We will not all sleep, but we will all be changed— [52]in a flash, in the twinkling of an eye, at the last trumpet. For the trumpet will sound, the dead will be raised imperishable, and we will be changed."

(1 Corinthians 15:51, 52)

Do you get the idea in these passages of Scriptures that there is a trumpet blast involved in the announcement of Christ's second coming? What is with that trumpet? When the children of Israel traveled with the tabernacle in the desert the Bible tells us that God would determine where, and for how long, they stayed in one place.

"Whenever the cloud lifted from above the Tent, the Israelites set out; wherever the cloud settled, the Israelites encamped. [18]At the LORD's command the Israelites set out, and at his command they encamped. As long as the cloud stayed over the tabernacle, they remained in camp. [19]When the cloud remained over the tabernacle a long time, the Israelites obeyed the LORD's order and did not set out."

(Numbers 9:17-19)

When God decided that it was time to break camp and march

to the next location he had the people summoned, assembled and told to march by using trumpets. It was like "Ready, set and march."

> **"The LORD said to Moses: [2] "Make two trumpets of hammered silver, and use them for calling the community together and for having the camps set out."**
> (Numbers 10:1,2)

Today we await only the last trumpet of God. We have already been told to have our house in order. We are to be prepared and live lives of readiness. The New Testament is filled with such admonitions. When Jesus returns there will only be one final trumpet, a heavenly summons, "March." The big three events yet to come are the second coming of Christ, the final judgment and the creation of the new heavens and the new earth where God will live with His people forever. Those three events are pictured in the final three feasts. Before we look at these final three feasts here is a chart which presents them in the same order they are found in Leviticus 23.

		Month		
1	PASSOVER	1	CHRIST'S DEATH ON THE CROSS	REDEMPTION
2	UNLEAVENED BREAD	1	SINLESS LAMB OF GOD	
3	FIRST FRUITS	1	RESURRECTION OF CHRIST	
4	WEEKS, PENTECOST	3	BIRTH OF THE CHURCH	
LONG INTERVAL				
5	TRUMPETS	7	SECOND COMING OF CHRIST	KINGDOM
6	DAY OF ATONEMENT	7	FINAL JUDGEMENT	
7	TABERNACLES	7	GOD WILL DWELL WITH HIS PEOPLE	

So, in the prophetic calendar of the Feasts of Israel, it is only fitting that the silence after the long gap should be broken with the blast of a trumpet.

The Last Trump (Feast 5 - Rosh Hashanah, The Feast of Trumpets)

This feast is described in Scripture as a time of blowing the trumpet. It was a call to repentance and worship. Jewish literature describes it as one of the Jewish Days of Awe, a time of preparation and introspection leading up the most solemn day of the year, The Day of Atonement (Feast 6).

> "23 The LORD said to Moses, 24 "Say to the Israelites: 'On the first day of the seventh month you are to have a day of rest, a sacred assembly commemorated with trumpet blasts. 25 Do no regular work, but present an offering made to the LORD by fire.' "
> (Leviticus 23:23-26)

To the people, Trumpets as a feast reminded them that they were the people of God, especially called out. It was a time to remember how God led them and it served as a hope that God would lead in the future. It was not just the beginning of the New Year on the Jewish calendar but it represented new hope.

One author penned these words about that hope:

> *"The scattered sons of Israel's race*
> *That trumpet's sound shall bring.*
> *Back to their land to know and claim*
> *Messiah as their King."* (Unknown)

The feast was celebrated in both solemnity and joy. The trumpet sound was viewed as a time to awaken from slumber and prepare hearts for the next feast, the Day of Atonement.

Streets of Sorrow (Feast 6 - Yom Kippur, The Day of Atonement

Yom Kippur or the Day of Atonement is the most solemn day of the year for the Jewish people. It has been that way since God instructed the children in the wilderness to observe it. On that day the high priest took off his colorful garments, only wearing his white undergarment like all the other priests. He then made a sin offering for himself before he did the same for the people. Then he entered the Holy of Holies covered in a cloud of incense and presented the blood of the sin offering at the Mercy Seat on the Ark of the Covenant. It was the only day of the year he could go beyond the veil. God would then meet with the high priest on behalf of the nation and accept the blood offered for the people. Meanwhile, the people outside prayed for God's forgiveness.

The lengthy sacrifice and cleansing rituals of Leviticus 16 leave a very strong and clear statement that to enter the presence of God is no small thing. The ugliness of sin and the holiness of God are central themes of this most solemn day. In all, it was a day of repentance, a day of introspection. This remains today the most important day of the year for the Jewish people, even for those who are not active in their faith on a regular basis.

I believe, along with many Bible scholars, that God will have one final Day of Atonement and bring a large remnant of believing Jews into the kingdom (Romans 11:25-27). Others don't see a future for Israel. But the shadow of Christ is the same no matter what a person believes about the future of national Israel. Christ is not only our High Priest but our sacrifice as well. Only the blood of God's acceptable sacrifice, His son, can ultimately atone for our sins, whether Jew or Gentile. No blood of bulls or calves nor good works can make a man right with God. Faith in God's way of salvation, the blood of Christ, is the only way our sins can be forgiven. Any other way and we are left standing on the wrong side of the veil. For those, the words of Revelation chapter 20 will come to pass.

> **"Then I saw a great white throne and him who was seated on it. Earth and sky fled from his presence, and there was no place for them. [12]And I saw the dead, great and small, standing before the throne, and books were opened. Another book was opened, which is the book of life. The dead were judged according to what they had done as recorded in the books. [13]The sea gave up the dead that were in it, and death and Hades gave up the dead that were in them, and each person was judged according to what he had done. [14]Then death and Hades were thrown into the lake of fire. The lake of fire is the second death. [15]If anyone's name was not found written in the book of life, he was thrown into the lake of fire."**
>
> (Revelation 20:11-15)

But for all who have found their Day of Atonement then the final feast of Israel will have personal meaning. It looks forward to the day when God will live with His redeemed people on a new earth.

Streets of Gold (Feast 7 – The Feast of Tabernacles)

When the solemn Day of Atonement was over the next feast was already in preparation, the Feast of Tabernacles. The actual title for the entire final three-feast season is the Feast of Tabernacles or Booths. This last feast is a celebration. The children wandering in the desert looked forward to the day when the pilgrimage would be over and they would live in the land of promise with their God. In the desert God provided water, food and manna for His people and then He fulfilled His promise by bringing them to their own land. The celebration of Tabernacles lasted eight days. Even today many people in Israel celebrate the feast by moving out of their homes and living in temporary tents to remember the wilderness experience of their ancestors. All the time they anticipate the day when Messiah will ultimately dwell with His people in the land of promise.

> "Then I saw a new heaven and a new earth, for the first heaven and the first earth had passed away, and there was no longer any sea. ² And I saw the Holy City, the New Jerusalem, coming down out of heaven from God, prepared as a bride beautifully dressed for her husband. ³ And I heard a loud voice from the throne saying, "Now the dwelling of God is with men, and he will live with them. They will be his people, and God himself will be with them and be their God. ⁴ He

> will wipe every tear from their eyes. There will be no
> more death or mourning or crying or pain, for the old
> order of things has passed away."
>
> (Revelation 21:1-4)

One of the dramatic moments in the life of Christ took place
during a Feast of Tabernacles. It is found in the Gospel of John
chapter 7.

> "On the last and greatest day of the Feast, Jesus stood
> and said in a loud voice, "If anyone is thirsty, let him
> come to me and drink. [38]Whoever believes in me, as
> the Scripture has said, streams of living water will
> flow from within him." [39]By this he meant the Spirit,
> whom those who believed in him were later to re-
> ceive. Up to that time the Spirit had not been given,
> since Jesus had not yet been glorified. [40]On hearing
> his words, some of the people said, "Surely this man
> is the Prophet." [41]Others said, "He is the Christ."
>
> (John 7:37-41)

You might say Jesus broke up the party. The high priest had
just returned from the Pool of Siloam with a golden bowl and
poured water out at the base of the great sea, or laver, in the
temple courtyard. The people were singing the Hallel Psalm
"Blessed is he who comes in the name of the Lord" The water
was a reminder of how God brought water from the desert and
nourished His people. They all looked forward to the day when
the tyranny of Roman bondage would be broken and their God
would once again deliver them, live with them and supply all
their needs. It was at that moment that Jesus literally shouted
the words, "If anyone is thirsty, let him come to me and drink.

Whoever believes in Me, as the Scripture has said, streams of living water will flow from within him." It was a stunning moment, everyone froze. It was a claim that He was what the One the Feast of Tabernacles was all about. He was the end of the shadow.

The first sacrifices pointed to Him, the altars pointed to Him, the priests pointed to Him, the entire tabernacle and later the temple pointed to Him. Many events like the Exodus, the brazen serpent, the water from the rock and others pointed to Him. The prophets, the Psalms, the Law, the writings were about Him and His one unchanging plan of redemption for His broken world. It was all about grace and the love of God. And now we see the feasts of Israel were clearly about Him and His two-fold plan to redeem His people and to come back to get His stuff. Reading the entire Old Testament is like walking through a forest of shadows that all point to a lonely tree on a hill far away where the Prince of Glory died in our place.

God spoke clearly in the pages of the Old Testament say-ing, "I don't want you to miss this." Remember what He told those two on the Emmaus road:

> **"And beginning with Moses and all the Prophets, he explained to them what was said in all the Scriptures concerning himself."**
> (Luke 24:27)

Conclusion
OUT OF THE SHADOWS

I asked an artist what he sees when he does a charcoal drawing. Not being an artist myself I tend to see the bright things, the light first. But he told me he sees blocks of shadows. They define the image. He went on to say that you can't start with the details or you will lose proportion. The shadows are the key to understanding the light and the details.

When I look at the Old Testament today I see the light because I see the shadows. I hope this little book helps you do the same. That is why I wrote it. I also hope you go back and read the passages in detail and marvel at the amount of information God gave about His Son in those early writings.

The conclusion I have come to over the years is that the people in the Old Testament were not only saved the same way we are, by grace through faith, but they had ample information at any time to understand their own sinfulness and God's provision of substitution and forgiveness. They knew more than we sometimes think they knew.

A Personal Story

Years ago I had an interesting event happen to me that illustrates salvation in the Old Testament. In the neighborhood where we lived there was a family of, well let's just say "bad characters." I was a firefighter at the time and was coming home from work after an all-night shift. As I turned onto our street, I saw the little boy, who lived in that house with his grandparents, driving a four-wheeled powered vehicle. He was too young to drive and quite irresponsible. As I approached my home, he almost ran into my car. I had to swerve to avoid him. It made me angry. The boy quickly drove to his house and ran around the back. I went to the house to let the family know that the boy about killed himself and damaged my car. I still had my uniform and badge on when I went to the door and rang the bell.

The grandfather opened the door. I was still upset when I began to tell him what had just happened. The grandmother also came into the conversation and acted like a mamma bear protecting its cub. The boy himself walked into the living room and the grandfather shouted to him asking if what I was saying had indeed just happened. The boy said, "He's lying grandpa, I never did that." The grandfather looked at me with rage and yelled at me to "get off his property." I was so upset that I said something that was quite out of character for me and something I would never have actually done. I told him the next time the boy drove at my car maybe I wouldn't stop. It was a stupid thing to say and it only angered the grandfather and grandmother even more. Needless to say, it was not a pretty picture. If I recall it was a Sunday morning and my worship experience that day was pretty useless. I was stirred up because of what had happened and what I had said.

Well, it was several months later that I resigned my career and left with my wife and our five children to attend Bible School. We had been planning for about a year to go into full time ministry and needed theological training. So we left for a three year time of study. During the second year we had a real revival hit the campus. I had never seen such a thing. I had only read about times like this. People were overcome with a strong sense of sin and repentance was the order of the day. It was like a huge wind that swept the campus; you could literally feel it in the air. I was hit with the full force myself. I still remember weeping in a service one night as I saw my sin and the pride in my life. It had become like a festering cancer in my soul. I knew I had to make a lot of things right with people I had hurt. Then God clearly brought to mind that incident with the boy who almost ran into me.

I still remember arguing with God. I said, "Yes, Lord, I said dumb things but that kid and that family were wrong. They are bad people, and they had no right to endanger my family or to call me a liar." It was like God said to me, "You sinned and you need to deal with your sin." I knew what I had to do. I knew I had to return to that family and apologize to them and ask

their forgiveness. I really did not want to do that and I struggled and struggled, justifying my behavior. After all, I reasoned,
they were really bad people. God's conviction only increased.

I reminded God that we were in Bible school in the middle of
a semester and the Bible school was 2,000 miles from that
family. God only increased the conviction level to the point that
I was almost sick to my stomach. I finally caved in. I couldn't
take it any more. I totally broke down and wept and wept. I
promised God that the next summer when we returned for
a visit to our hometown that the first thing I would do is go
to the family and apologize for my behavior. That was it. The
peace of God flooded my life. I felt like a million pound weight
was lifted off me. I knew God's forgiveness in a profound way.
God had broken his stubborn child and the joy I experienced
was overwhelming.

I actually never thought about that promise the rest of the
semester. I was forgiven and the forgiveness was real. The next
summer we drove down from the Bible school in Canada to our
home in California. About half way to our home the promise I
had made to God came back to my mind. God reminded me of
my oath. It actually stirred my soul again with some of those
feelings of resentment for that family. But I quickly told God
that I would do as I vowed as soon as we got there. When we
drove into our town and turned down that road my heart was
pounding in my chest. I stopped in front of the family's house
and prayed that they were not there or had moved. Actually I
really hoped they were in jail. Then I realized how stupid that
was and got out of the car. I walked up to the same door where

our angry confrontation had occurred. I swallowed hard and rang the doorbell.

A few moments later the door opened and it was the grandfather. I could see the rebellious kid and the momma bear standing a few feet away. All three were standing right there. There was silence for a few seconds. I said, "Do you remember me?" He said, "Oh, yeah, I remember you and . . ." I interrupted what he was going to say. "I just wanted to apologize for my behavior at your door the last time I was here. It was wrong what I said and I never should have come to your door angry and talked to you like that. My wife and I are Christians and God has convicted me of that sin and I want to ask your forgiveness for my actions that day." The grandmother immediately shouted at me, "Well, it's about time you finally grew up." I responded, "Yes, you are right. It's about time I grew up." At this point the grandfather had no idea how to handle this. He just stared and then started to fiddle around and stutter his words and basically said, Well maybe we all said things that. . . "I cut in again. "Sir, I can only deal with my part in this event. I was wrong and it has nothing to do with whatever anyone else did. I was wrong and I just wanted you to know that." He accepted my apology and I left. But when I left I felt that same relief and joy I had experienced when I first obeyed God and was forgiven many months earlier at Bible School.

My forgiveness was real when I first confessed my sin before God. But that forgiveness was based on something that was still to happen. I had not actually gone to the family and made it right. So, in a sense you could say I was forgiven on credit. I still had to pay for the crime by apologizing. But before that could happen I experienced a real joy and forgiveness based on what was yet to happen.

The Old Testament sinners who repented found real forgiveness and real relationship with God even though it was based on an event yet to happen. How real was the salvation of those in the Old Testament? It was as real as the promise of God that He would send His son to pay for those sins. The promise was a certainty. So, they were, like me, saved by credit based on the fact that God would take care of the sin issue later in history. God accepted the faith and obedience of His erring children and forgave them based on what Jesus would one day do on the cross.

Today we live after the shadows. We have the Light Himself and if we know Him as Savior we will live in the light forever. I trust you have made that eternal decision. If you haven't, now would be a great time to leave the shadows and come to the light. How? Simply ask Him to forgive you and commit your life to follow Him. You will find that He changes lives. He always has whenever anyone comes in faith and surrenders to Him. He is still the patient Father waiting for His prodigals to come home!

"... he got up and went to his father. "But while he was still a long way off, his father saw him and was filled with compassion for him; he ran to his son, threw his arms around him and kissed him.

²¹"The son said to him, 'Father, I have sinned against heaven and against you. I am no longer worthy to be called your son.'

²²"But the father said to his servants, 'Quick! Bring the best robe and put it on him. Put a ring on his finger and sandals on his feet. ²³Bring the fattened calf and kill it. Let's have a feast and celebrate. ²⁴For this son of mine was dead and is alive again; he was lost and is found.' So they began to celebrate."

(Luke 15:20-24)

Conclusion